From the Ground Up

A Workbook On Coalition Building and Community Development

Edited by:
Gillian Kaye and Tom Wolff, Ph.D.

Contributions from:
David Chavis, Ph.D.
Stephen Fawcett, Ph.D.
David Foster, Ph.D.
Vincent Francisco, Ph.D.
Beth Rosenthal, M.S.

Layout and Design:
Christine Driscoll

Supported by the W.K. Kellogg Foundation

Tom Wolff

5th Printing Spring 2012
TomWolff & Associates
24 South Prospect Street
Amherst, MA 01002
Phone:413-253-2646
tom@tomwolff.com
www.tomwolff.com

First printing 1996

Fourth printing 2002

Fifth printing 2012

Fifth printing Spring 2012
Tom Wolff & Associates
24 South Prospect Street
Amherst, MA 01002
Phone:413-253-2646
tom@tomwolff.com
www.tomwolff.com

Printed and bound in the United States of America

Layout and Design: Christine Driscoll

Printing and Binding: United Book Press

ISBN: 0-9678782-0-9

Acknowledgments

There are many people, directly and indirectly, who have been enormously helpful in developing this workbook:

Christine Driscoll, AHEC/Community Partners
Linda Gross, AHEC/Community Partners
Nancy Barrett, AHEC/Community Partners
Beth Rosenthal, M.S.
Steve Fawcett, Ph.D. The Work Group on Health Promotion and Community Development
Vince Francisco, Ph.D. The Work Group on Health Promotion and Community Development
Adrienne Paine Andrews, Ph.D. The Work Group on Health Promotion and Community Development
David Chavis, Ph.D.
David Foster, Ph.D.
Neil Novik, Berkshire AHEC
Mick Huppert, University of Massachusetts Medical Center Office of Community Programs

Gillian Kaye and Tom Wolff, Editors

Contents

Introduction

In the Spring of 1993, the W.K. Kellogg Foundation asked us to put together a three day workshop for many of the projects funded by the Health Section of the Foundation. These projects are innovative approaches to community-based health issues, and were, in general, characterized as grassroots groups attempting to tackle the major health and quality of life issues in their communities. At the core of the many approaches were interventions involving coalition building and community development. Thus the workshop focused on these issues. As a result of the success of this workshop the Foundation asked us to put our material in Workbook form, for a more general audience, and that is what follows. We assume that some readers will read this Workbook from cover to cover. But most will see it as a helpful resource to look at a Chapter at time.

Coalition building and community development are two powerful interventions to create healthy communities. Both interventions are complex, community-wide processes that often that often proceed in fits and starts. This Workbook is an attempt to share with practitioners in the field some ideas, some frameworks, some exercises that have evolved from the work of the authors in communities across the country. Our goal is to keep each Chapter brief, and to provide, where appropriate, worksheets at the end of chapters that individuals and their communities can use to examine their existing efforts and find ways to improve them. At the end of each Chapter are Resources and References related to that topic, and the final Chapter of the Workbook lists more general resource books and papers with an annotated description.

In Chapter 1, Tom Wolff describes some of the crises facing our communities today and articulates the goal for most community development and coalition building, which is building healthy communities. That system of health and human services which exists in every community is assumed to be the community and the government's response to the problems in that community. However, as he notes in this Chapter, there are many shortcomings to that system, and coalition building becomes one route for creating more competent helping systems.

In chapter 2, Tom takes a careful look at the assumptions underlying coalition building, and clarifies what a coalition is, what is collaboration, and what is empowerment. With the onslaught of coalitions for every topic imaginable occurring in our communities, those of us who are committed to an empowerment approach must help define what the criteria are that will truly make a coalition an empowering intervention.

Chapter 3 spells out the principles of success for building community coalitions. Here, Tom Wolff and David Foster lay out a series of principles that are generally applicable to all coalitions, and are drawn from over ten years of coalition building experience in over a dozen different communities. These principles include not only the obvious, such as a clear coalition mission and goals, and strong leadership, but also a need for hope, celebration, time and persistence.

The process of coalition development is not without conflict and difficulties, and in Chapter 4, Tom Wolff illustrates a range of barriers that are typically presented for those trying to create coalitions in communities. Too often, when people experience these barriers, they feel it to be a personal shortcoming. They say to themselves, "If only we had a better coalition coordinator, we wouldn't be having all these turf barriers among partners." In this Chapter, Tom suggests that turf battles are an expected and normal event in coalitions development. We need to understand and appreciate such barriers, and develop appropriate strategies and interventions to overcome them.

The demographic move to diversity that this country is experiencing is also a major factor in coalition building and community development interventions. In Chapter 5, Beth Rosenthal assesses the issue of multicultural coalitions, and articulates a range of barriers that are likely to occur, and many important strategies that a coalition can use to prevent difficulties from occurring while supporting multicultural coalition development.

In Chapter 6, Beth goes on to deal with the issue of conflict in coalitions. As opposed to avoiding or denying conflict, Beth not only suggests that we deal with it, but implies that a healthy coalition needs to have some love for conflict in order to deal with the inevitable numbers of conflicts that will come to its door. Coalition building and community development are, by definition, attempts to shake up the normal way of doing business. Thus, the fact that conflict is encountered is inevitable. Beth provides a wonderful framework for categorizing and finding creative and successful approaches to dealing with conflicts as they emerge in coalition development.

Involving grassroots citizens in the work of coalitions is one of the thorniest issues that coalitions grapple with. Again and again, we hear coalitions bemoan the lack of real citizens and residents as participants in their coalition efforts. In Chapter 7, Gillian Kaye spells out a clear framework and many helpful suggestions for involving and mobilizing the grassroots. The outreach strategies she suggests are well tested approaches that have successfully engaged citizens in community-wide efforts.

Gillian Kaye and David Chavis continue on the theme of developing community involvement in Chapter 8, where they spell out an innovative community assessment technique that is a key tool for involving and mobilizing the grassroots. This social reconnaissance approach is a community-wide intervention, involving all sectors of a community in naming, understanding and acting upon the major issues that face the community. Again, this is a well tested technique that has worked in both rural and urban areas and provided both a wonderful "kickoff" for community development efforts and a solid base for building community support.

In Chapter 9, Gillian Kaye attempts to help you put it all together with the development of action plans for your community coalition. Drawing from materials in the preceding Chapters, Gillian lays out a typical coalition planning process, and leads you step-by-step through developing an action plan for your own coalition based on a self-assessment of the many issues discussed in the Workbook. The final action plan can be the most important outcome of your involvement with this Workbook. It is our hope that readers will take both ideas, and most importantly the Worksheets, back to their own coalitions, and involve the coalition in self-assessment and self-examination that will help it move forward in more effective ways than ever before.

In Chapter 10, Steve Fawcett, David Foster and Vince Francisco spell out a monitoring and evaluation system for coalitions that helps to answer some of the key process and outcome questions that occur in community-based efforts. Too often, the practitioners who are implementing coalition building and community development efforts are convinced of the powerful impact they are having, but are unable to show it to their own members, the community-at-large, politicians or funders. Fawcett, Foster and Francisco explain a practical method for monitoring and evaluating the process and outcome of coalition efforts. This system, which has been used with both specifically targeted coalitions (i.e., teen pregnancy, substance abuse) and more general, community-wide coalitions, provides regular feedback to the coalition on how it is proceeding, and a clear enough picture of outcomes to help funders understand the value of their investment.

Finally, Chapter 11 contains a brief annotated bibliography of a few especially helpful resource manuals which every coalition needs to know about.

♦Eds.

CHAPTER 1

Coalition Building: One Path to Empowered and Healthy Communities

by Tom Wolff, Ph.D.

Contents

Problems Facing American Communities

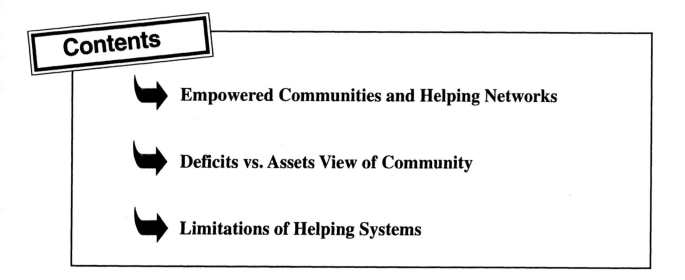

American communities are struggling with issues of citizen participation, intolerance, violence and a sense of powerlessness. There is a need to develop interventions to create competent and empowered communities. These include competent helping systems and empowered and mobilized citizens. Coalition building and community development are reemerging as techniques to enhance the quality of life in our communities. To start our workbook we need to revisit the difficulties our communities are facing and the limitations of our present helping system.

In our experience, both communities and citizens report feeling helpless and unable to do anything about their situations. They are disenfranchised—powerless—often both as individuals and as whole communities. It is not easy for these citizens to realize that they can have an impact on their lives or their communities. These conditions recall those reported by Saul Alinsky over twenty-five years ago:

"In our modern civilization, multitudes of our people have been condemned to anonymity—to living the kind of life where many of them neither know nor care about their own neighbors—millions of our people know deep down in their heart of hearts that there is no place for them—that they do not count. They have no voice of their own, no organization to represent them, no way in which they may lay their hand and their heart to the shaping of their own destinies."

What is less obvious, but also illustrative of the struggle for a livable community, is the difficulty engaging citizens to participate in their own communities, schools, and neighborhoods. Yet we know that we cannot solve the complex problems facing our communities without active involvement of all parts of our community. There are also a growing number of reports of intolerance of diversity in any form: racial, sexual, religious, or ethnic. Our communities cannot seem to embrace all their citizens as equal members.

Our Goal: Healthy And Empowered Communities

In light of the above, a move to systematically build empowered and competent communities is needed. But what is a healthy, empowered and competent community? Here are some ideas about what a healthier community might be:

❑ Ira Iscoe defines a competent community as "One that utilizes, develops or otherwise obtains resources—including the full development of human resources." An empowered community is one that is able to gain mastery over its life.

❑ The World Health Organization's use of the concept of "healthy cities" provides another view of competent and empowered communities. According to Len Duhl, a healthy city or a healthy community is one "that is continually creating and improving those physical and social environments and expanding those community resources which enable people to mutually support each other in performing all the functions of life and developing to their maximum potential."

❑ Trevor Hancock states that the prerequisites for health include: "A just, equitable society, a sustainable ecological system, peace, shelter, food, education, and income."

In the author's view, an empowered community has two components: first, a competent helping system, including both formal and informal elements; and second, an empowered and mobilized citizenry. An empowered community would thus have both individuals and a community as a whole capable of gaining mastery over their lives.

Pathways To Healthy, Empowered and Competent Communities

If we are to create competent helping networks and empowered communities in the 1990's, we will need to create new responses to service system difficulties. This will require a paradigm shift—a new way of looking at our world. This new view will be built upon a set of key concepts—coalition building, empowerment, and community development. Coalition building produces one pathway to creating more competent helping systems in communities.

In almost any community, from small rural mill towns to large urban centers, there exist multi-million dollar health and human service systems which include everything from daycare to welfare, a social service system to mental health clinics, to nursing homes to hospitals to parks and recreation departments. These services carry a joint mission of improving the quality of life for the citizens in their communities. Despite the millions of dollars spent on this mission in any single community, there is generally not a single dollar nor one entity responsible for overseeing this system and trying to make sense of it. And as we have tried to make sense of the community's helping networks, we began to understand that there were significant shortcomings in the whole system.

Deficits Versus Assets View of Community

Our understanding of the major difficulties in these helping systems has been strongly influenced by the work of John McKnight, and how his writings correspond with what we are being told by people in the community. McKnight suggests that professional human service approaches overemphasize the deficits and needs of individuals and communities rather than their assets and capacities.

He says the helping system works like a reverse job interview. You come to me for an interview, and I say o.k, I want to know all your problems - financial, health, social, family, historical, etc. And the more problems you have, the higher salary I'm going to offer you for the job. Ever been to a job interview like that? This author doesn't remember one, but that's the way our human service system works. And we see it so clearly when we go into communities and we say, "what are the issues in this community?" The human services and others quickly raise their hands and say all the horrible things that are happening — unemployment, poverty, child abuse, domestic violence, drugs, etc. We have a dozen communities in Massachusetts who all claim to have the worst teen pregnancy rate in the state. What an honor. Our system seemingly demands that people present this deficit view. As an alternative, McKnight suggests that when we assess communities we look at communities in terms of their assets rather than their deficits.

We see frequent examples of McKnight's critique in our communities. In one community, we met with a junior high school principal because there was a significant amount of conflict between students in the school. A number of parents suggested that the school implement a mediation program and use student mediators. The principal explained to the parents the developmental limitations of these adolescents (their children) and how they would be totally incapable of being mediators. Despite the principal's objections, three years later, trained student mediators are in the school doing quite well. But that perception of the deficits as opposed to capacities (in this case of the students) is resonated time and time again by many in our helping systems.

McKnight also suggests that the health and human service systems "push out the problem solving actions of friend, neighbor, citizen and association," and that "as the power of professionals and service systems ascend, the legitimacy, capacity and authority of citizens and community descends." These statements resonate with what Seymour Sarason called the "Anarchist Insight," that as government programs increase, no matter how well intentioned, they rob people of the psychological sense of community and weaken a community's sense of responsibility.

Finally, McKnight suggests that it isn't until the capacities of people are recognized, honored, respected and lifted up that outside resources make much difference. The appropriate role for the helping system might be that of nurturing the "community way" — the natural mechanisms by which communities support themselves and the individuals within them. This can be done by assuming that citizens are experts and the system isn't, by finding out who is solving problems and how they are doing it, and by conducting asset surveys instead of needs assessments. Ultimately, McKnight believes in eliminating the helping system, and that the "community way" can and will take over. Our work does not reinforce his extremist position.

Although we agree with McKnight's critique of the present helping system, we believe that he romanticizes the capacity of communities to manage these very difficult problems totally on their own. We are looking, in our work, for a marriage of a new service system and the community way, and are, for the moment, experimenting with what that relationship might look like.

Dealing With Diversity

A second major difficulty that we have found in community helping systems is the inability of helping systems to deal with issues of diversity. These systems too often rely on modes of service delivery that were developed by white, middle class males and may be quite inappropriate when applied to most other populations. When agencies try to deal with expanding access to these services to diverse populations, they usually take the existing models to new geographic or ethnic communities.

But recognizing cultural diversity means much more than delivering traditional models in new locales. It means that a competent system will develop alternative modes of delivery that are culturally relevant to the needs of the various racial and ethnic populations of that community, and will develop these in partnership with these communities. We have a wonderful example of that in the Latino Community in Holyoke, Massachusetts. They are trying to deal with issues of teen pregnancy and noticed that many of the teenage mothers avoided seeking prenatal care at area clinics. These teens had come from Puerto Rico, where going to a high tech clinic was a sign that there was something medically wrong with the pregnancy. Service providers needed to de-stigmatize the way of getting information and services to these teen mothers. In response, they developed a program called CEDE which sets up "charlas" (house chats) and resource centers in community apartments. These programs allow women to get the needed information and increase their capacity to access services without having to go to a high tech clinic. This is an example of developing alternative delivery systems that are culturally relevant.

Inefficiencies And Incompetence In The Helping System

Our final observations regarding helping systems deal with the numerous inefficiencies and incompetencies in the system that seriously limit its overall effectiveness.

❑ Duplication of Effort

Duplication of effort, not duplication of service, occurs when various groups within the community work to solve the same problem without talking to each other. For example, a group in a church concerned about teen pregnancy, a group at Family Planning concerned about teen pregnancy and another one in the schools all meet without knowing that the other groups exist. This happens again and again. Then, when a group comes forth with its recommendations, they are surprised to find out there is another, similar group in existence.

❑ Fragmentation

Another issue with helping systems is that they are very fragmented. Agencies receive categorical funding and then tend to look at individuals in a very fragmented way. I once presented a hypothetical case to a group of community service providers. In this case a 22 year old woman arrives at an agency's door, her 3 and 5 year old children with her. She moved out of her apartment to flee from her physically abusive husband. She reports a drinking problem, financial problems, difficulty finding work, fear that her husband will find her and beat her and fear that she might lose control with her own children. I asked each agency to think about how they would see her. They reported the following: one agency saw her as a problem drinker, another as a displaced homemaker, the third as a child abuser, a fourth as a victim of domestic violence, a fifth as an oppressed woman, and a sixth as a general anxiety disorder. None of them seemingly could see her in all these ways. It was not because of the intellectual limitation of the professionals, or their values, but the way the system is set up and the way they are funded and the way they ended up having to deal with the citizens who come to their door.

❑ Competition

A third component of the issue of efficiency and effectiveness is the focus on competition versus cooperation and collaboration. In many states and communities there exists an overtly competitive environment where health and human service agencies actively compete with each other for clients and resources. A recent example shows the absurdity of this. In one community we work with, there were two mental health agencies which, because of financial pressures in the human service business, considered merging. The merger attempts failed bitterly. The two agencies then competed for a number of service contracts that were split between them. Now, the mental health clients in that community go to one provider for their psychotherapy and another for their medication. The belief that the staffs of these agencies will work together well after such a bitter battle is naive.

❑ Lack of Planning

Finally, and most profoundly in our experience, is that there is often no capacity to plan for the issues that are coming to the community's door. This lack of planning is especially true when you look at new, emerging issues. We saw it around homelessness and we saw it around HIV. Now, as we are beginning to face the epidemic of violence in communities, there's no way to have everyone in the community look at these new issues and try to pull their thoughts and actions together. Planning is usually lacking within both individual agencies and state systems, since each tend to act in a "demand" or crisis mode.

Our coalition building work has attempted to assist the helping systems to function more competently and we have defined that as: coordinated, holistic, planned, accessible, collaborative, preventive, comprehensive, and culturally relevant. They provide accessible information, emphasize the community's assets, deal with emergent problems, and maximize both formal and informal helping. When competent, these helping systems are integrated into the community to promote the individual and community's capacity to solve its own problems.

Table 1 summarizes our concerns with the present helping system and suggests examples of goals and coalition building tactics that can lead to change.

Table 1

Service System Concerns and Community Goals, and Coalition Building Tactics

Concerns with the Health and Human Service System	Community Goals	Examples of Coalition Building Tactics
1. Duplication of effort	Coordination	Information sharing meetings Problem solving task forces Service guides
2. Fragmentation of services	Systemic/ holistic approach	Comprehensive services Protocols Collaboration
3. Competition	Cooperation	Problem solving task forces Topic-focused monthly meetings Develop resources for collaborative
4. Crisis orientation/ remediation	Prevention	Develop new prevention projects Coordinate existing prevention efforts Elicit community support for prevention
5. Multicultural insensitivity	Culturally relevant services	Develop coalitions in communities of color Challenge larger system to address issues of cultural relevance

6. Excessive professionalism	Integration of formal and informal helping network	Create ways to meaningfully involve clergy, business, and citizens Bring formal and informal providers together Neighborhood organizing
7. Limited and inaccessible information	Effective and accessible communication	Coalition newsletters, service guides Work with media Create settings to encourage members to get to know each other
8. Lack of planning	Long-term planning	Systemic identification of priority issues Problem solving task forces on current and emerging issues Regular review of issues, goals and plans
9. Inequality	Equal access	Advocacy for change of state/local programs Address barriers by developing new systems
10. Detachment from community and clients	Connection to the community	Bring community and providers together Involve community in defining issues, gathering data and mobilizing resources

Conclusion

Our communities are struggling and our usual helping system responses are not a match for the community's problems. There is a need to reexamine our traditional helping systems so that they can be more responsive and appropriate. Coalition building and community development approaches as spelled out in the following chapters of this workbook offer new ways to create healthy communities.

Key Points

- Empowered communities have two essential components: a competent helping system that includes formal and informal elements and an empowered and mobilized citizenry.

- Professional human service approaches often overemphasize the deficits and needs of individuals and communities rather than their assets and capabilities. These approaches crowd citizens out of the process of defining solutions and strategies. While it is not true that citizens are the only experts, a marriage must be found between the service system and the "community way" of assessing and solving problems so there is a partnership between the two.

- Helping systems have difficulty dealing with issues of diversity. There is a need to change modes of service delivery that were developed for white, middle class populations to respond to new, diverse groups. Recognizing diversity means developing alternative modes of delivery that are culturally relevant to the needs of racial and ethnic populations in the community.

- Duplication of effort, fragmentation and competition in our service systems severely limit our competency and effectiveness. We must seek a coordinated, holistic, planned, accessible, collaborative, preventive, comprehensive and culturally relevant approach to our systems that maximize both formal and informal helping.

Resources and References

Alinsky, S. (1989). Statement Industrial Area Foundation, in S. Horwitt, Let Them Call Me Rebel, New York: Knopf, p. 105.

Duhl, L. (1990). The Social Entrepreneurship of Change. New York, NY: Pace University Press.

Hancock, T. (1991). Healthy Cities: The Case of Canada. Presented at conference Building Health Through Community, Boston, April 1991.

Iscoe, I. (1974). Community psychology and the competent community. American Psychologist, 29, 607-613.

McKnight, J. (1990). Address to New Haven Foundation, New Haven, November 1990.

McKnight, J. (1989) Do No Harm: Policy options that meet human needs. Social Policy, 5-15.

Sarason, S. (1976). Community psychology and the anarchist insight. American Journal of Community Psychology. 4: 243-261.

Worksheet #1

Clarifying Your Coalition's Agenda

Instructions:

Check off which of the following are part of your coalition's agenda. Discuss with the whole group.

❑ **Information sharing/networking**

>Among providers

>With community

❑ **Lend support to projects of individual members**

❑ **Problem solving/conflict resolution**

>Among members

>Between members and community

❑ **Multi-member collaborations**

>Coordinate existing services

>Develop new resources for new services

❑ **Coalition-wide collaborations**

>Service planning

>Advocacy

>Outreach

>Provider/community education

❑ **System/community change**

CHAPTER 2

Coalition Building: Is this really empowerment?

by Tom Wolff, Ph.D.

Contents

- What is a coalition?
- What is collaboration?
- What is empowerment?
- Comparing community based and community development approaches
- Coalition empowerment self assessment process

The language and practice of health and human services in the 1990's is dominated by two catch phrases: coalition building and empowerment. Both words are used loosely; they are not very well defined and are frequently linked together. We see funding initiatives from federal, state and local governments and from private foundations that urge applications involving coalition building as a method to empower. This combination of two unclear phrases can lead to even more misunderstanding and potentially misdirected programming in our communities.

Many of us have seen this mismatched pair of phrases go astray in coalitions in our communities. Some examples include:

- A minority coalition gets linked to a community health center to apply for a federal minority health grant. When the dollars arrive, the minority health coalition gets left out of staff hiring, and only select members of the Coalition become members of the health center advisory board to the project. The coalition splits from the health center. Is this coalition building? Is this empowerment?

- A substance abuse prevention coalition decides to expand its mission to focus on minority substance abuse issues by applying for a Center for Substance Abuse Prevention (CSAP) Community Partnership grant. It turns to the minority community for support of its application. When in turn the minority community requests that the Board of the Fighting Back agency have more minority representation, it labels the request a "terrorist action." Is this coalition building? Is this empowerment?

- A substance abuse treatment agency becomes the lead agency for a CSAP Partnership, with a focus on empowerment. As the agency experiences financial difficulty, it taps into over $100,000 of the CSAP funds to cover its own debts. When it finally goes bankrupt, the CSAP Partnership is $100,000 short. Is this coalition building? Is this empowerment?

- A coalition engages in a visioning exercise. As they envision the state of the community in 10 years, someone asks how many of those in the room live in the community. Less than 1/2 of those in the room are residents, yet they are designing the community's future. Is this empowerment? Is this coalition building?

I am sure that there are many stories that each of you can relate that raise some of the same questions. The first step in bringing clarity to these issues requires defining both terms.

What Is A Coalition?

There are many definitions of coalitions, let's look at a few:

- Cheri Brown defines a coalition as, "An organization of diverse interest groups that combine their human and material resources to effect a specific change the members are unable to bring about independently."

❑ Ron LaBonte suggests that coalitions are, "Groups of groups with a shared goal and some awareness that 'united we stand, and divided we fall.'"

❑ Feigherty and Rogers differentiate coalitions three ways based on their membership—grassroots, professional, and community based.

What Is Collaboration?

Coalitions are generally aimed at trying to promote collaboration, and this word can also be a nightmare to define. Arthur Himmelman suggests that coalition building can have as its goal simply **networking**, which is often defined as exchanging information. Or **coordination**, which is exchanging information and creating activities for mutual benefit. Or **cooperation**, which involves sharing resources for mutual benefit to achieve a common purpose. They are not always aimed at the most comprehensive form of partnership, which is defined as **collaboration**.

❑ The National Assembly of National Voluntary Health and Social Welfare Organizations suggests that collaboration is, "The process by which several agencies or organizations make a formal, sustained commitment to work together to accomplish a common mission. Collaborations require a commitment to participate in shared decision making and allocation of resources related to activities responding to mutually identified needs."

❑ Arthur Himmelman defines collaboration as a "voluntary, strategic alliance of public, private and nonprofit organizations to enhance each other's capacity to achieve a common purpose by sharing risks, responsibilities, resources and rewards."

What Is Empowerment?

There are numerous definitions of empowerment as well, some follow:

❑ In its simplest form, empowerment is defined by Meredith Minkler as "The process by which individuals and communities gain mastery over their lives."

❑ The Cornell Empowerment Group states that "Empowerment is

an intentional, ongoing process centered in the local community, involving mutual respect, critical reflection, caring and group participation through which people lacking an equal share of valued resources gain greater access to and control over those resources."

- ❑ Nina Wallerstein states that "Empowerment is a social action process that promotes participation of people, organizations and communities toward the goals of increased individual and community control, political efficacy, improved quality of community life and social justice." She points out that most commonly, the term empowerment is used as an individual term, but her work expands the definition to include organizational and community empowerment.

But we need to truly understand the consequences of talking about empowerment. Empowerment calls for a fundamental shift in power. Ron LaBonte says, "Empowerment is a noble word, but the reality of political and economic distribution of power does not yield win-win scenarios. Socially disadvantaged communities empower themselves, in part, by reducing the constraints imposed upon them by wealthier and more powerful interests." This is a key aspect of real empowerment. He raises concerns that, given the prominence of empowerment in discussing health promotion, it is surprising how little the concept of power has been addressed.

Community Based Versus Community Development

Given the range of definitions of the terms coalition building and empowerment, how do we differentiate and understand the relationship of these two terms to our coalitions? Two models are especially helpful in allowing coalitions to examine their own assumptions. David Chavis and Paul Florin differentiate between **community based** and **community development** approaches. And Arthur Himmelman distinguishes between **collaborative betterment** and **collaborative empowerment**. All of these terms and perspectives allow us to see some of the assumptions and values that underline these approaches and can help us assess whether our coalitions are promoting empowerment or not.

Chavis and Florin note that most coalition building efforts can be divided into two approaches—community based vs. community development. They point out that these approaches represent opposite ends of a continuum and elements of each can be present in any given program. Both approaches have value, however, the community development approach is based more clearly on empowering the community.

• The *basis* of the **community based** approach is a focus on weaknesses, and solving problems by addressing deficits. The **community development** approach builds on strengths and competencies.

• The *definition of a problem* in a **community based** approach is made by agencies, government, and outside institutions, while in the **community development** approach the community defines the problem.

• The primary *vehicles for creating change* in the **community based** approach are information, education and improved services, whereas the **community development** approach involves building community control and increasing community capacity.

• In a **community based** approach, the *professionals* are the key and central decision makers, whereas, in a **community development** approach, the professionals are a resource to the community's problem solving.

• The *primary decision makers* in a **community based** model are the agency and government representatives and other appointed leaders. In the **community development** model the key decisions are made by the indigenous, informal and elected leaders from the community.

Collaborative Betterment vs. Collaborative Empowerment

Arthur Himmelman arrives at a very similar understanding in differentiating the terms collaborative betterment and collaborative empowerment. Both are forms of what he calls multi-sector collaboration, that is partnership across various parts of the community. Himmelman notes that, "The ownership of any social change process is among the most, if not the most important of its characteristics. Ownership is a reflection of a community's capacity for self-determination and can be enhanced or limited depending upon how collaboration is designed and implemented." He compares betterment and empowerment initiatives.

• First, he asks *who starts the coalition.* If it started outside the community, it's a collaborative betterment process, if it started from inside the community, it is a collaborative empowerment process.

• In the collaborative betterment process, the *role of the community* is to be invited in; whereas in a collaborative empowerment process the community is central to the effort and is the starter.

• Who *controls the decisions* again differentiates: in collaborative betterment efforts large institutions are in control, while with collaborative empowerment it is the community.

• The *outcomes* of the collaborative betterment process are policy changes and improved program delivery and services. Whereas the outcomes of the collaborative empowerment process include both those things accomplished in collaborative betterment plus, long term ownership and enhanced community capacity for self determination.

Both Chavis and Florin and Himmelman point out that the empowerment-community development approach leads to increases both in community ownership and in individual and community control over its own destiny.

Assessing Empowerment

So, for those who wish to do coalition building to promote empowerment, and for those who wish to fund coalition building to promote empowerment, how do we differentiate various community efforts? How can we assess our partnerships and collaborative efforts in terms of their empowerment potential?

Chapter 1 suggests that coalition building as one path to empowered communities holds great hope for building healthy communities that have both competent and responsive helping systems and an empowered and mobilized citizenry. However, if coalition building is used to describe mergers of health and human service programs in the quest to become mega-agencies and empowerment is used to describe attempts by human service providers from outside the community to design services for local citizens, then we will have undermined the great potential inherent in both these approaches.

This chapter proposes a self-assessment process to allow coalitions to determine their present status in relationship to the processes and outcomes of empowerment. Not all coalitions are committed to empowerment. There are many legitimate definitions of coalition, and many coalitions are committed to specifically increasing the competence of health and human service systems. However, many coalitions attempt to include empowerment in their vision, and for those that do, this self-assessment process has been designed as a way to gauge how well they are reaching that end.

The self-assessment Worksheets following this chapter cover: goals and objectives, membership, communication, decision making, leadership and leadership development, use of resources, coalition activities and coalition outcomes.

Conclusion

Coalition building holds great promise as a technology to help communities foster empowerment. But not all coalition building efforts are truly committed to empowerment. For those that are committed to empowerment, we have created criteria to assess that commitment. The Coalition Empowerment Self-Assessment Process that follows proposes a beginning set of criteria to assist coalitions in examining the depth and clarity of their commitment to empowerment both as a process and an outcome.

Key Points

- Coalitions are diverse groups that combine their resources to create change.
- Empowerment is the way that individuals and communities gain mastery over their lives.
- Empowerment is a struggle.
- Coalitions need to be clear whether their goals are to create "betterment" or empowerment.

Resources and References

Brown, Cheri (1984). The Art of Coalition Building. New York, NY: American Jewish Committee.

Chavis, D., and Florin, P. (1990). Community Development, Community Participation. San Jose, CA: Prevention Office, Bureau of Drug Abuse Services.

Cornell University Empowerment Group, (1989). Networking Bulletin: Empowerment and Family Support. Vol. 1, Issue 1, October, 1989.

Feigherty, E. and Rogers, T. (1990). Building and Maintaining Effective Coalitions. Palo Alto, CA: Health Promotion Resource Center, Stanford University School of Medicine.

Himmelman, Arthur. (1992). Communities Working Collaboratively for a Change. Monograph. Minneapolis, MN: The Himmelman Consulting Group.

Labonte, R. (1989). Community empowerment: The need for political analysis. Canadian Journal of Public Health, 80, 87-88.

Labonte, R. (1993). Health Promotion and Empowerment: Practice Frameworks. #3, Toronto, Ontario, Canada: University of Toronto, Centre for Health Promotion.

National Assembly of National Voluntary Health and Social Welfare Organizations, The. (1991). The Community Collaboration Manual. Washington, DC.

McKnight, J. (1989). Do No Harm: Policy options that meet human needs. Social Policy, Summer, 5-15.

Minkler, M. (1989). Health education, health promotion and the open society: An historical perspective. Health Education Quarterly, 16, 17-30.

Wallerstein, Nina. (1992). Powerless, Empowerment and Health: Implications for health promotion programs. American Journal of Health Promotion, 6, #3, 197-201.

Wolff, T. (1992). Coalition Building: One path to empowered communities. Monograph. Amherst, MA: AHEC/Community Partners.

Worksheet #1

Question I - Goals and Objectives
The first critical question is whether empowerment is a stated goal of the coalition. Often it is an implied goal of the coalition, one assumed by many members but never stated. Or else it can be a stated goal of the funder and may be included in the funding application but not in the ultimate goals of the coalition.

1. How do your goals and objectives clearly demonstrate that empowerment is one of your desired outcomes of the coalition?

2. Which specific objectives translate empowerment into more specific terms? Are you working toward leadership development, advocacy, increased capacity of communities or individuals to solve their own problems, etc.?

3. If empowerment is a stated goal, how is empowerment defined, and WHO is to be empowered (citizens, agencies, government, business)?

A coalition that is serious about creating empowerment outcomes and process will include empowerment in its goals and objectives, and will clearly and specifically define both what they mean by empowerment and who will be empowered.

Worksheet #2

Question II - Membership
Coalition membership will vary in part depending on how seriously a coalition takes its commitment to empowerment.

1. In what ways is membership inclusive or exclusive? Who can or cannot join?

2. What, if any, are the financial barriers to membership? For example, does someone have to pay or appeal for scholarships to join?

3. Describe the diversity of the coalition's membership (for example: geographic, racial, ethnic, economic). What sectors of the community are represented in the coalition (educational, religious, business, law enforcement, media, health and human services, neighborhood/citizen groups)?

4. In what ways are explicit attempts made to engage citizens in the coalition? What role do citizens have in the coalition? How is this role stated in the coalition's goals and objectives? At what level(s) and in which ways do citizens and citizen groups actually participate in the coalition?

Coalitions that wish to be successful at accomplishing empowerment goals need to have open and inclusive membership; limit barriers to coalition membership for all citizens; be diverse and multisectoral; and, most importantly, have citizen and citizen group membership in the coalition.

Worksheet #3

Question III - Communication

1. How and to what extent is information on coalition activities and decision-making distributed? What information do new people receive that makes them feel part of the group quickly?

2. How can actual community citizens access coalition information?

3. How does the coalition use the media to inform others who are not in the coalition?

4. In what languages are meetings and materials presented? Does this give adequate accessibility to members of the coalition and the citizens of the community?

Himmelman (1992) points out that the degree to which, "language, data, information and other forms of communication encourage grassroots participation" is critical to collaborative efforts being successful in their pursuit of empowerment.

Worksheet #4

Question IV - Decision Making

Himmelman (1992) and Chavis and Florin (1990) all indicate that the degree to which, "those most affected by the collaborative mission, goals and actions shape the mission, goals and action" is critical to a coalition process being an empowerment process.

1. How are key coalition decisions made? Are they made by the people most affected by the decisions? These decisions include, at least: coalition start up, coalition ending, designing coalition activities, allocation of resources, hiring of staff.

2. How is the decision-making process spelled out? Is it in writing? Is it understood and accepted by all in the community?

3. Is decision making in the hands of a few individuals or a single individual; or is there broader power sharing around decisions?

4. If a subgroup (a steering committee or a coalition coordinator) makes decisions for the coalition, is that group democratically chosen and representative of the community?

5. What is the organizational chart for the coalition? How much does it represent a typical hierarchical organization versus a more lateral organization that spreads out decision-making, power, communication, etc.?

A critical question in decision-making centers on who is a "representative of the community." In coalitions defined by geography it is critical to clearly define what it means to be a representative of the community. Being a citizen or resident of the community is generally the core criteria for defining community representatives. Although this may seem obvious, we often see coalitions where people who provide services within the community but live elsewhere are designated as representatives of the community. The bottom line in assessing a coalition's commitment to empowered decision-making is whether those most affected by the decisions are the key architects of the decisions.

Worksheet #5

Question V - Leadership and Leadership Development
In coalitions committed to empowerment the opportunities for coalition leadership and the efforts at leadership development are critical. Empowerment involves a process of working WITH people rather than doing FOR people. Thus leadership issues are paramount to the reality of a coalition's commitment to empowerment. If the coalition leadership roles are filled with all the 'same old faces,' then one can see that leadership development is not occurring.

1. Is coalition leadership confined to an individual or a small handful of individuals? Are there more professionals or citizens in leadership roles?

2. How do new members of the coalition take leadership roles?

3. Is leadership limited to individuals because of age, gender, race, religion, ethnicity, or class? (Do women, people of color, and low income people hold leadership positions?)

4. In what ways has the coalition made an explicit commitment to leadership development of citizens and residents? Are there plans and resources to implement such leadership development? Describe them.

Coalitions that promote empowerment create leadership opportunities for all coalition members and actively commit themselves to the development of new leaders, not just in the Coalition, but throughout the community — leaders from low income populations, from minority groups, from neighborhoods, and among youth.

Worksheet #6

Question VI - Use of Resources

Money talks. How a coalition uses its resources is an excellent indication of its commitment to empowerment. Resources means not only dollars, but also access to training, travel, consultation, literature, and special events.

1. Does everyone have access to coalition resources or are they only available to a small handful of people who have certain connections?

2. Who controls decisions concerning the use of coalition resources?

3. Towards what use is coalition funding put? Is it committed to expanding the effectiveness of the coalition in its catalyst role, or to utilizing the coalition as a program developer? If the coalition runs programs, do these programs have empowerment goals?

4. Do the long term resources generated by the coalition benefit those who did not initially have access to them? [Himmelman (1992)] In what ways?

The use of money and other resources in a coalition can be very telling regarding commitment to empowerment. Coalitions that use their resources to become service providers, especially of services that are not focused on empowerment, may be no different than any other human service agency. McKnight's (1989) critique of service providing suggests that professional human service approaches overemphasize the deficits and needs of individuals and communities rather than their assets and capacities. He states that, "as the power of professionals and service systems ascend, the legitimacy, capacity and authority of citizens and community descends." (1989)
If a coalition is committed to empowering the community then the allocation of resources should reflect that commitment.

Worksheet #7

Question VII - Coalition Activities

Fawcett (1991) points out that a coalition's commitment to empowerment is evident in coalition activities. Only some coalitions take community actions that occur outside the coalition and attempt to change community policies, practices or programs related to the coalition's goals.

1. Does the coalition take actions outside of the coalition in order to create community changes? What are these actions?

2. Does the coalition provide community organizing and education activities? In what ways?

3. Does the coalition engage in advocacy? Describe some activities.

4. Does the coalition have a relationship with local government officials — city, town, state, federal? How does the coalition advocate for the needs of citizens or agencies in these relationships?

The extent to which the activities of the coalition reflect empowerment outcomes is a critical differentiating point. Coalitions that claim to focus on empowerment, but essentially provide services that support the status quo service delivery model, are not necessarily empowering coalitions.

Worksheet #8

Question VIII - Coalition Outcomes

The proof is in the pudding. If coalitions are committed to empowerment then the coalition outcomes should reflect this priority. If all a coalition can claim as its successes are programs designed and implemented by professionals then the empowerment commitment must be questioned.

1. Are community groups and individuals better able to address and resolve their concerns? In what ways?

2. Is there an increase in citizen participation in any aspect of community life? Describe some of the increases. Have more citizen leaders emerged?

3. Do citizens report a greater sense of community? Give some examples of this increased sense of community and how it was achieved.

4. In what ways do citizens and the community at large have access and control over more resources to meet their needs?

5. Has the quality of life in the community improved? In what ways?

Although increases in empowering processes are important, the ultimate (and often long term) empowerment outcomes are the critical measures of whether the original empowerment goals and objectives have been achieved.

CHAPTER 3

Principles of Success in Building Community Coalitions

by Tom Wolff & David Foster

Contents

It is a considerable challenge to derive a general set of principles for successful coalition development in light of the great variation in what is called a 'coalition.' The definitions of coalition vary widely, from two agencies joining together in a grant submission to acquire money, to a broad community group with representatives from every sector working to improve the community. How coalitions define 'success' will also vary from coalition to coalition, and over time within a coalition (e.g., we have succeeded if we get the Chief of Police to join our coalition vs. we have succeeded if we get the Chief of Police fired).

From our experiences, we have learned about many aspects of coalition development. We have reported these lessons in a number of publications, including a series of Tip Sheets on coalition building, several of which are referenced below.

Assumptions

To clarify the principles of success in a brief chapter, it is necessary to first spell out some of the basic assumptions of the particular approach to coalition building articulated in this model:

1. **Ecological approach**: Individuals are understood in the broadest context of their environment. Thus, when examining social problems (e.g., drug abuse, teen pregnancy) always consider the major forces in American life today that impact on the problem including: racism, sexism, class elitism, and social and economic injustices.
2. **Social change**: Coalitions are committed to addressing those components of society that require change as opposed to simply improving ways to adapt to society's ills.
3. **Multisectoral-multicultural approaches**: Coalitions need to be open to everyone in a community. The coalitions' basic principles must celebrate diversity and must value the multicultural characteristics of their communities. Institutional racism needs to be identified and addressed. In communities of color, empowerment within their own community may need to precede multicultural efforts.
4. **Capacity approach**: Coalitions focus on their communities' capacities and strengths as well as their deficits and problems. They focus on individuals as citizen rather than, or as well as, clients.

Principles

We have organized the principles of success in eight broad areas. Many of them will seem obvious—true for many types of organizations. In our experience guiding and supporting the development of an array of coalitions, the usefulness of these principles has been consistently reaffirmed. However, in the development of many coalitions, they are frequently overlooked. This may be due, in part, to the fact that many coalition participants are used to operating in top-down organizations with missions, structures and resources heavily influenced by outside forces, particularly funding sources.

Mission and Goals

Coalition members must clearly define their shared mission/goals and assure that the identified goals incorporate the self-interests of the various constituencies, plus something larger than those self-interests. Coalition building requires both a realistic understanding that addressing the self-interests of participants is crucial, and a willingness to set aside personal agendas for a common good. Walking the tight rope between these agendas is critical to coalition success.

When a coalition includes large numbers of health and human service providers, it is common to find some tension about the mission of a broad-based coalition. There are members who believe the focus of the group should be on improving the system of services through increased communication, coordination and collaboration. There are others whose concerns are focused more on advocating for, and guiding, social change in collaboration with non-providers in the community. While these are quite different agendas representing different self-interests, coalitions are able to bridge them by openly acknowledging the differences and creating working groups within the coalition that address each area of concern. The mission statements and goals may reflect this dual approach explicitly.

Inclusive Membership

Membership in a coalition needs to be inclusive, allowing all members of a community who endorse the coalition's mission to join in the coalition's efforts. Inclusive membership will occur only through active recruiting of the two power extremes in the community—the most powerful (business, clergy, city hall, etc.) and the least powerful (neighborhood groups, youth, people of color, the poor, etc.). The geographic boundaries of the coalition will also be decided by those directly involved.

There are really two issues lodged within this principle. First, are the definition and structure of membership open and inclusive? There are coalitions that define membership as being specific representatives, or their designees, from particular organizations and/ or constituencies. It is tempting to do this to keep the group small and more efficient, or to assure participation of important leaders and gain in efficiency. Within any community there is a wealth of talent and wisdom—among professionals, residents, and others—that is inevitably lost when membership is "by invitation only." Coalitions composed of the already influential can effectively exert one kind of power, but it is rarely about social change. It most often deals with symptoms, not the root issues. It also rarely succeeds in mobilizing the community to address fundamental community issues. (See Chapter 5 for more details on multicultural issues in coalitions.)

The second issue: Are there specific goals and strategies to reach out and engage those who are not ordinarily welcomed to these kinds of community efforts? This is not as easy as it sounds, particularly the strategies. Coalitions that want to actively involve both residents and professionals must resolve a variety of barriers: When will the coalition meet, during the day or in the evening? Will the location, process, language and agenda be ones that are welcoming and comfortable for all groups? In diverse communities, how will the cultural and linguistic issues be addressed? These are but a few of the challenges to building truly inclusive coalitions. The obstacles are real, but our experience shows that there are substantial benefits to working thoughtfully and openly toward overcoming them. (See Chapter 7 for more details on mobilizing and involving the grassroots).

Organizational Competence

The group's organizational structure and modes of operation must be clear and competent enough so that the coalition can perform basic tasks effectively. Five key elements include: leadership, decision making, communication, resources and staffing.

Leadership

Coalitions need to have a clearly identified leadership structure, but also need to disperse leadership as broadly as possible. Within coalitions, the most effective leadership is that which focuses on facilitation and coordination. When those who are used to being in charge of a traditional organization assume leadership of a coalition, it is useful to adopt a somewhat different style, so as to invite broad participation and greater engagement. As we note in Chapter 5, leadership is also a key aspect of creating a multicultural coalition.

Building new leadership is a crucial role for coalitions. Often we see those who lead the coalitions feeling overloaded with the responsibilities of committees and projects, on top of the work they are getting paid to do. It usually takes an intentional plan, endorsed by these multi-role leaders, to identify and nurture others in the coalition with interests and abilities for assuming increasing responsibilities within the group. This need is especially great among community groups which have been disenfranchised, where leadership potential has been largely discounted and discouraged: communities of color, women, youth.

Decision Making

A clear, democratic decision-making process is needed which allows for broad participation in determining the course of the coalition. Where there are leaders wanting (or even willing) to control the decision making, the coalition needs structures that assure a democratic process. Coalitions should be thoughtful about how, and what, authority is delegated to Executive Committees or officers, and how they are accountable to the whole. This is true even when current leaders are seen as "trustworthy"—both because the way decision-making power is shared sends messages about the coalition's values, and because who is leading is more likely to change than the process.

In addition to structures for basic decision making, it is helpful for coalitions to allow for conflict and disagreement to occur and be resolved within the 'normal' processes. We find that many coalition leaders, particularly among professionals, experience conflict as negative and detrimental to the group. Their first instinct, therefore, is to making decisions in a way that glosses over areas of disagreement, rather than recognizing and learning from them. (See Chapter 6 for more on dealing with conflict).

Communication

Active and effective communication among members of the coalition, and between the coalition and both the community and outside system (e.g., the State), is critical. All of these are a challenge for most coalitions. They take time; they require a clear sense of what message the coalition wishes to send to its members, to the community and to others. Some coalitions have developed effective monthly newsletters—from four to a dozen pages—to disseminate the news, ideas, requests, etc. that they want to share with an array of audiences. Minutes of coalition meetings and short committee reports included in the newsletter are more likely to be read, and more economical to distribute. We have found that sometimes this newsletter helps people feel like members of the group even though they may be able to attend only occasional meetings. It also keeps the coalition in the eyes of elected officials and other leaders who may not be directly a part of the group.

Resources

The mobilization and effective use of resources from within the coalition, and outside, is essential. Our monitoring and evaluation research suggests, however, that while critical resources can be a boon to the coalition, they also can create serious difficulties. We have observed several coalitions in which the pursuit of, the decision making about, and management of financial resources severely weakened the coalitions. This was generally because these issues about funds distracted the group, or at least the leaders, from the work of building a strong organization and being clear about the coalitions' purposes and plans.

We would caution coalitions about going after resources, even for staffing, until there has been some time to: (1) build relationships, (2) define initial agreements about mission and goals, and (3) establish some track record of small successes for the group as a whole. From this base, the coalition can both more safely and more successfully seek funding for staffing to support the work of the group.

Staffing

Most broad-based coalition efforts benefit significantly from having experienced staff and consultants. The staff must have good group and organizational process skills and community development philosophy and skills. The appropriate type and best use of staff resources is a critical issue. Some coalitions see a staff person as a guide, facilitator, problem solver and communications link. Others see having staff as a way for coalition members to avoid having to do the essential volunteer work. Like the nonprofit model, the members become a "board" that sets the agenda for the staff to carry out. This latter approach undermines the essential collaborative, community building functions of the coalition, as we have defined them.

In addition to these professional functions of staff, many coalitions benefit from the work of clerical staff, either hired or donated. Such staff can be responsible for compiling and sending out mailings, setting up meetings and making follow-up calls in support of the coalition leaders. This will increase volunteers' willingness to serve in leadership roles and enable them to focus more on the process and productivity of the group.

Services from an experienced consultant/resource person from outside the group can also bring several benefits. First is the lessons learned from other coalitions in the practical matters of coalition building. Second is a neutral, facilitative role to help the group with problem solving and planning. In both processes, it is sometimes helpful to have facilitation from someone who is not part of the group's ongoing issues and to allow the coalition's leaders to step back and participate as members of the group.

Planning

With coalitions, as with any complex organization, good planning increases the chances for success. Thus they must develop at least a rudimentary system for ongoing planning. While this may seem obvious, we have observed that left to their own devices, many coalitions do not do systematic planning. When encouraged to, however, most coalitions do so with very positive results.

We have found that an annual, half-day, all-coalition planning meeting is one useful catalyst for successful planning. The meeting format which we have developed has four components.

• Review

The first is a review of the coalition's work since the previous planning meeting (for new coalitions, a reflection on their process of coming together). This includes naming accomplishments, identifying the benefits of participating in the coalitions, and articulating the frustrations or disappointments members have felt.

• Reassessment

The second is reassessment of the coalition's organizational development. The group reviews issues of leadership, committee structure and effectiveness, assesses the flow of communication, and considers issues related to membership—diversity, outreach, participation and support. This is a chance to consider if the people who "should" be around the table are there, and if not—why not; and, whether those who are members are contributing their time, skills and organizational resources to support the work of the coalition, and if not—why not.

- Plans

Third, the group focuses on how these reflections and other available information can guide what the coalition plans to do in the coming year, and how it should organize that work. This part of the meeting identifies the community and coalition issues that might be addressed during the coming year, establishes the coalition's priorities, and determines how to organize the working groups needed to effectively address these issues. It is important in defining these issues that several things be considered: Is the issue focused and specific enough to allow the group to have a direct impact? Are there real chances for some success in the near future? Is there an adequate group of coalition members committed to working on this issue?

- Next Steps

The final component is to develop specific work plans that identify the next steps: What needs to be done? By whom? By when? There is real benefit in having those attending the planning meeting get to this level of development, usually by breaking up into working groups, but there is often insufficient time. When that is the case, we recommend that work groups use the end of the meeting to schedule their next group meeting and commit to bringing their work plan to share at the next coalition meeting. This helps assure that the momentum of the planning meeting will be maintained and there is some accountability for each group to define a specific plan for action.

Action and Advocacy

Successful coalitions take actions that are doable and thus prove their effectiveness to themselves and their communities through concrete results. This often means that coalitions choose promising projects for success to guarantee early victories that will illustrate to the members and the communities that change can occur. A short agenda of doable tasks also prevents a coalition from spreading itself too thin.

With a solid base in group process and planning, coalitions need to be action oriented to produce meaningful change. While networking and information exchange are valuable underpinnings for the coalition, specific actions need to emerge from the planning that are targeted to achieve coalition goals in the community. Our data shows clearly a direct benefit from planning, which leads to community-oriented action, which yields community changes. While not necessarily sufficient, each is necessary for the next.

One lesson we derive from this is that in their early development coalitions should not expect to, or be expected to, produce significant changes (outcomes, impacts) in short periods of time. If there is pressure for immediate results, planning will be shortchanged, actions may not be carefully conceived, and the long term results will likely suffer. Short term visible outcomes available to coalitions include: creation of a newsletter, creation of a service guide, meeting with the Mayor, or a legislative breakfast.

Advocacy, defined as actions targeted to produce specific organizational or community changes, is an essential part of any effective action plan. There are many forms that this advocacy may take—public or private; in-person or written; individual, small group or large group; etc. This may vary based on the style of the group, the particular "target", or the nature of the issue. Coalitions committed to success and change must expect to engage in advocacy. To avoid advocacy, as some coalitions do, is to severely limit the potential impact of the coalition.

Hope and Celebration

Coalition activities need to include fun and must affirm the strengths and joys of the community. Indeed, one of the great gifts of effective coalitions to their members and to their communities is the gift of hope that emerges from an optimistic coalition approach that affirms that many community problems can be effectively addressed. Leaders will promote the hope and accomplishments of the coalition, helping the group celebrate this process.

The vitality and morale of a coalition is noticeably enhanced when it remembers to celebrate its successes. With the many challenges that confront most coalitions, it is easy to get mired in the work of dealing with all that has yet to be done and the burden of more demands than can be met. In the face of this, many coalitions forget to step back and reflect publicly on the groups' accomplishments.

Annual meetings are one vehicle that coalitions use to set time aside for this purpose. Public recognition of these achievements can be enhanced by using coalition newsletters, public meetings and the local media. Awards to coalition members and community members are also key to celebration.

Time and Persistence

The agendas of broad-based coalitions that address the quality of life in communities can be overwhelming. The coalition needs to take a long-range view, understanding that successfully tackling its agenda will take time and persistence. Although some single issue coalitions are defined as short-term efforts, the coalitions described in this model will create the desired societal changes only within longer time frames. Taking on big issues in manageable pieces is a strategy for success in both long- and short-term efforts.

How often we find coalitions being pushed, both by funders and from within, to produce results quickly. As a society we are increasingly addicted to the "quick fix," and our tolerance for long-term, developmental or preventive approaches is low. Coalitions face the challenge of producing some short-term products without turning away from the long-term commitment and strategies that hold the greatest promise for building healthier communities.

Monitoring and Assessment

The process of developing an effective coalition to address quality of life issues in a community is obviously very complex. While the literature can provide us with some direction, each coalition's efforts must be guided by its own internal review and evaluation process. Whether this review is done at an annual meeting discussion of the coalition's process and outcomes— or through a more rigorous evaluation scheme, an effective coalition needs to have the capacity to learn from its successes and its disappointments, for it surely will have both.

Chapter 10 on Monitoring and Evaluation of Coalitions describes one approach to this process. It uses several tools: a logging system for accumulating and graphing information about coalition actions and outcomes; a Membership Satisfaction Survey; and a Critical Events Report. While each of these can be used independently, together they offer views of the group from three complementary perspectives.

Conclusion

The growth and development of each community coalition is unique, depending on its membership, its purpose and its context. It is also a complex process which is difficult to fully capture. As our experience with, and study of, coalitions grows, however, we discover increasing commonalities across many types of coalitions. Some lessons address how to adapt basic organizational development and group process principles to the coalition context; while others relate to the specific "life history" of coalitions.

The above principles are a 'work in progress.' We hope they can be used as helpful hypotheses to be tested in various communities.

Key Points

- In order to succeed, coalitions need to have a clear mission and inclusive membership.
- Coalitions, like all organizations, must be able to handle key organizational issues, such as: leadership, communication, conflict, decision making, staffing and resources.
- Successful coalitions must be committed to action and advocacy.
- The coalition process is slow and requires time and persistence, promoting hope and celebration, and keeping members engaged and encouraged during the process.

CHAPTER 4

Barriers To Coalition Building and Strategies To Overcome Them

by Tom Wolff, Ph.D.

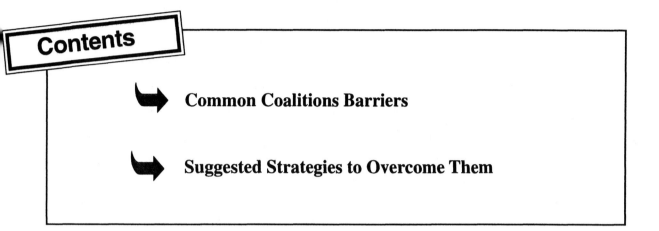

Contents

Anyone who has been in a coalition will tell you that the path to success is a rocky one, often marked by two steps forward and one step back. This shouldn't surprise us! As we have already noted, there are many forces in communities and community helping systems that are opposed to coalition building and community development. If we think about the path of a coalition's development as being guided by forces that are at work promoting successful coalition building, and barriers that exist or are created to that coalition building, then we can understand the process as being a dynamic one, one that is constantly changing with time. In this chapter, we will look at the nine most commonly encountered barriers to coalition success, and outline some strategies that a coalition might develop to counteract them.

Barrier 1—Turf and Competition

A clear and explicit goal of coalitions is often to promote coordination, cooperation and collaboration. It comes as no surprise that **turf, territoriality and competition among coalition members** is a major barrier to coalition success. The capacity of one organization to feel competitive with another often amazes outsiders. This competition can be just within health and human service agencies as they compete for clients and contracts, but can also be between the schools and human service agencies, between the private sector and the public sector, between the city/town government and state government, and between local government and the community. A new contract to provide a service might be issued by the state, and two or three different agencies, all members of the same coalition, begin to compete for that contract, seemingly undermining the coalition's goal of cooperation. One would hope that, having declared themselves wanting to be a part of a coalition, these territory battles would decline, but often they escalate instead. The arrival of a coalition itself can be seen as competition. People will tell you, "Our agency already calls a meeting for those people who serve children, we don't need a new coalition in town."

Strategies

In his community organizing work, Saul Alinsky always paid attention to the self interest of all the parties, believing that the solutions had to include attention to the self interest of all. Too often we expect self-sacrifice from individuals and organizations as they move toward coalition solutions. If we understand that people and organization's self-interest is part of the reality and may be part of what motivates people, then we can approach this situation by looking for strategies around turf and territoriality that take into consideration self-interest. It is also possible to minimize the impact of turf, territoriality and self-interest by appealing to a larger good. In our experience with coalitions, the larger and common good that has most appeal is that of community and neighborhood. This is why coalition building often focuses on geographic areas.

Barrier 2—Bad History

The most frequent comment we get when we come into new communities and talk about building a new health and human service coalition or community coalition is, "Oh, we tried that once before here, it doesn't work." **Most communities have had unsuccessful attempts at building cooperation and coalitions over time**. Most frequently these attempts have been ill-fated because they did not involve a carefully thought out process, did not have enough resources to succeed, were imposed from above as a mandate, "You WILL cooperate," or the coalition was formed around an external mandate that declares, "You have a problem with teen pregnancy, we are going to give you money to combat this problem, but you need to create a coalition to get the money."

Conflictual histories also exist between agencies and different components in communities, and one should never forget the impact of historical conflicts. Too often we enter communities in an out-of-context way, thinking that history starts when we put our foot in the door. We should never forget the power of history. All we have to do is talk to an agency director and hear, "We don't work with that other agency because 15 years ago they had a director who insulted our director at a public meeting" to realize the powerful impact of history.

Strategies

The first strategy is to take a careful history of the community. Determine what efforts occurred in the past to try to build coalitions and cooperations and how they succeeded and failed. Also, one can collect a detailed history of conflict and cooperation between agencies in the community. Following that, the second key way to undo bad history is to create an open and fair process that allows everyone to participate, everyone to set the ground rules, and for everyone to set the agenda of the coalition. In this way, some of the factors that have led to conflict in the past can be avoided in this new round of coalition building.

Barrier 3—Failure To Act

One of the most "lethal" behaviors of coalitions is the endless, long-term planning meetings that a coalition can get bogged down in before they act. Many of us have sat on coalitions that aim to solve problems by involving a large number of important people with busy schedules who sit around a room for over a year; thinking, planning, doing needs assessments, before anything happens. In most cases, this long planning process without action is not only unnecessary, but can also destroy a coalition before it starts. Administrators and bureaucrats, are used to sitting in long-term planning meetings; even the best of them have a tolerance for them. But citizens, citizen groups, and those in the community committed to change are often quickly turned off by such an atmosphere. Coalitions at their heart are based on creating change and demonstrating the capacity to act. It is this capacity that attract the kinds of members who make coalitions succeed. When coalitions fail to display a commitment to action, or display a fear of advocacy, then they discourage the involvement of exactly these kind of people who will make the coalition a success. In order to keep key players in the coalition from the start, the coalition must be able to demonstrate a commitment to action.

Strategies

Although a coalition must be able to operate in a planful manner, it must also be able to produce some actions and results in its first weeks and months of existence. These are not opposite goals. One can be involved in a careful, long-term planning process, while at the same time, the coalition can act specifically on issues like creating a newsletter, circulating a petition at a coalition meeting, or holding a public session on a controversial topic, all of which can happen within the first months of a coalition's existence. It is these latter actions that show the membership and the community that the coalition is committed to making something happen, as opposed to writing reports that sit on someone's shelves. This commitment to action must be sustained throughout the history of the coalition, and indeed the monitoring and evaluation system described in Chapter 10 is a helpful way for a coalition to see whether its community actions are occurring on a regular basis.

Barrier 4—Dominance By Professionals

The key professionals in communities are critical members of most coalitions, and are often helpful assets. **Professionals can become a barrier when they dominate the process in such a manner that most of the membership is professional, the view of the community is only generated by professionals, and the control of the coalition is in the hands of professional agencies.** As we noted in Chapters 1 and 2, John McKnight criticizes professionals for focusing on a community's deficits. This can be illustrated by an example of an attempt to create a Teen Center. Adult service providers decided that one way to combat teen problems was by creating a youth center. They went about designing and opening this teen center without any input from teens. Then, when no teens showed up, the professionals blame teen apathy and teen problems for the failure, rather than recognizing that only by consulting with teens, and letting them decide how to best set up the teen center, could it succeed. This happens much too frequently, not only by individual agencies, but by coalitions of professionals.

Strategies

Active attempts to recruit citizens from the community are critical to the success of coalitions. We also respect the important role that 'citizen helpers' have. These are people who have professional roles in communities, but who are also active citizens of that community, and therefore can wear both hats. Having citizen helpers does not eliminate the need to have citizen members who are not helpers. When this is not possible, the coalition must get involved in soliciting ideas from citizens, to work with other citizens to "test out" new ideas before they are implemented. Unless the coalition is constantly asking the community what it wants, and then responding to that, it will not be able to overcome the dominance of both professionals and professional models.

Barrier 5—Poor Links To The Community

The majority of coalitions seem to have little success in establishing solid links to the community as a whole. By the very nature of coalitions that begin with gatherings of human service providers or educators, the meetings that are scheduled become inaccessible to working citizens in terms of time, space, and the language and culture of the meetings. When a group of individuals sit down and talk about the varied funding sources coming from the state, using a variety of acronyms and initials, ordinary citizens quickly understand that this is a world that they are not a part of, and don't understand.

Strategies

Obvious strategies not only include making meetings more accessible in terms of language, time, space, child care; but also having the agenda and process be citizen driven. David Chavis has suggested that most of the basic institutions in our community have become unaccountable to their citizenry; that the clergy is separated from its congregation, the schools from its parents and students, the health and human service system from its clients and patients. Rebuilding these links, and the accountability of the systems to the citizens is a critical piece of coalition work.

In some ways, it seems that the major strategy has to be an investment of funding into identifying and supporting and, if they are missing, creating citizen advocacy groups so that citizens can come to the table as representatives of constituencies like everyone else. In many communities, these citizen and neighborhood groups are there. Sometimes in a vibrant form, sometimes in a dormant form. In other communities, funding and staffing may be needed to develop these organizations.

Barrier 6—Minimal Organizational Capacity

There are numerous ways in which coalitions can fail at being healthy learning environments and organizations. These include unclear goals and objectives, inability to plan, poor information flow, lack of attention to maintenance tasks, and failure to provide leadership. Organizational capacity is critical to coalition success, but since it is covered elsewhere in the workbook, it will only be referenced here. These issues are covered in more detail in other chapters.

Strategies

The development of a clear and competent organization is critical for coalition success, one that has clear goals, a planning capacity, and where information flows readily, that attends to the maintenance task of the coalition, and where leadership is evident and widespread. Read about some concrete ways to achieve a "competent" organization in Chapters 3 and 5.

Barrier 7—Funding—Too Much Or Too Little

Most discussions of funding and coalitions deal solely with the issue of how to find funding to sustain coalition groups. **We would like to ask the question, "Is funding really needed for coalition development?"** It is interesting to compare coalitions that were started by grassroots groups with no money, versus coalitions that were gathered specifically around a funding source. In those coalitions that gathered around a grassroots community issue, whether it is substance abuse, violence, or teen pregnancy, we see genuine community interest at the outset. Often, they have little or no money. When we contrast that with those coalitions that were started by the potential lure of dollars, we do not necessarily see a great level of community involvement. There is no question that some community coalitions have been highly successful with virtually no funding. We have also seen very well funded coalitions (one might suggest, over-funded) fail. This raises fundamental questions about whether funding is always required for coalitions—and, if so, how much, what is it used for, and what are the kinds of problems, dilemmas, strengths and resources that are created by funding.

Funding can be a barrier for a number of reasons. Once a coalition gets into the business of delivering programming itself, or subcontracting out dollars for programming to other agencies, it runs the risk of moving from a collaborative organization whose sole function is to promote coordination and collaboration to becoming another community agency. This can create a conflict where the coalition is in competition with its own members.

Also risky is subcontracting program dollars to other agencies by coalitions. When a coalition does this, it needs to engage in a process of awarding and then monitoring the contracts. Subsequently, the coalition as a coordinating body also becomes a monitor of its own members, which creates an inordinately complex set of roles. In our experience, one set of functions often interferes with the other, meaning it is hard to be a collaborative partner with an agency if you are also monitoring a subcontract and potentially telling them that they are not doing a good job!

When coalitions are gathered together around the lure of external funding sources, one can never be sure that the partners at the table are not there just for the dollars. This leads to great ambiguity in the start-up of these coalitions. The best one can hope for is an open discussion of what brings people to the coalition table.

When a coalition gets involved with significant funds it sometimes finds a lead agency to handle these dollars rather than just a fiscal conduit or financial manager. The lead agency may then take on roles, responsibilities and power that place it on an unequal basis with other coalition members. Since one of the core premises of coalitions is that all members come to the table with equal power in the coalition, this can create difficulties.

Strategies

In our experience, we have seen the full spectrum—coalitions that had virtually no money, a moderate amount of resources to sustain the coalition efforts, or those with large amounts of resources to both sustain coalition efforts and develop community programming—be both successful and unsuccessful. Funding in and of itself does not guarantee success or failure, but the degree of funding and the way in which decisions about the funding are made, create very different sorts of organizations.

Coalitions often need a certain amount of funding just to sustain their basic efforts of coordination, collaboration and information exchange. The "basics" include money for mailings, agendas, rental of meeting space, and enough money for an annual meeting. The next increase of funding for coalitions often pays for part-time or full-time secretarial support to do the clerical work that goes along with coalitions: mailings, minutes, newsletters, etc. Many coalitions also see the need for more skilled staff to assist with coalition planning, direction, leadership, facilitation, or mediation. After funding for the basics, and potential funding for staff, the next direction for coalition funds is specific programming. The programs developed: substance abuse prevention, teen pregnancy prevention, tobacco cessation, etc. are often determined by the availability of a particular funding source. Our experience suggests that when funding is obtained for coalitions it is best first spent on basics, then staffing, and finally programming.

Core funding for staffing and maintaining the process and development of the coalition is critical for the success of most coalitions. It is our belief that, although unstaffed coalitions can be successful to some degree, the capacity of the coalitions to take on multiple issues over a long period of time and have a significant impact can be increased with paid, facilitative coalition staff. Thus, finding the resources to fund such staff is enormously helpful. Even a halftime staff person and secretarial support can be enough to move a coalition forward in a rapid fashion.

Barrier 8—Failure To Provide And Create Leadership

Coalitions have two leadership missions. One is to provide competent leadership for the coalition and its tasks, and the other is to create new leadership in all sectors of the community. Many coalitions fail at one or both of these missions.

There are coalitions where there is a lack of leadership—many lieutenants but no generals—and the coalition seems to flounder and not head in any one direction or accomplish any one task. On the flip side, we see coalitions with a single, dominant leader, who does not delegate, who does everything, and, as with any other organization, we find that the members and followers feel powerless and excluded. One of the problems of funding a staff person or more than one staff member for a coalition, can be that these paid individuals take on all the leadership roles, and members can easily say, "Well, I don't need to do that, we'll let our staff person do that." The creation of that kind of staff role then implicitly undermines the creation of new leadership roles among members.

Strategies

Coalitions must consciously foster the development of leadership among all its members for coalition tasks and to seek out new individuals to take leadership roles in the community. Leadership must be seen as multifaceted and occurring in many ways, not just who runs the meeting, or chairs a task force, but also who volunteers to get people to come to a meeting, or to set up refreshments for a meeting, or be the person who behind the scenes makes things work. Each of these are leadership roles. For more concrete strategies on leadership development, see Chapter 3.

Barrier 9—The Costs Outweigh The Benefits

The bottom line for participation in a coalition by any given member is that the benefits which they receive for participating outweigh the cost of participating. When one attempts to engage very busy members of a community in a coalition effort, it becomes a very delicate line to walk. Many coalitions fail when the costs of participation (especially time) greatly outweigh the benefits of being part of the coalition.

Strategies

Since what those costs and benefits are vary enormously from individual to individual and community to community, it is up to the coalition to do a careful assessment of what people are looking for, and to stay in touch with whether they are getting it. When that is done, the coalition can try to make the cost/benefit ratios favorable, and sustain coalition involvement by its members.

Resources and References

Alinsky, Saul. (1971) Rules For Radicals. New York: Random House.

Chavis, D., and Florin, P. (1990). Community Development, Community Participation. San Jose, CA: Prevention Office, Bureau of Drug Abuse Services.

Worksheet #1

IDENTIFYING BARRIERS TO SUCCESS IN YOUR COALITION

Instructions:

For each of the coalition barriers listed below, indicate examples of how it affects your coalition. Refer to the chapter text to clarify the barrier definition. Then brainstorm some ideas about how to address the barriers. Discuss what you have written down. This exercise can be done individually or in a small group.

Barriers | Potential Strategies

1. Turf and Competition

2. Bad History

3. Failure to Act

4. Dominance by Professionals

5. Poor Links to the Community

6. Minimal Organizational Capacity

7. Funding — Too Much or Too Little

8. Failure to Provide and Create Leadership

9. The Costs Outweigh The Benefits

CHAPTER 5

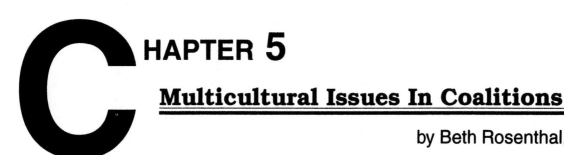

Multicultural Issues In Coalitions

by Beth Rosenthal, M.S.

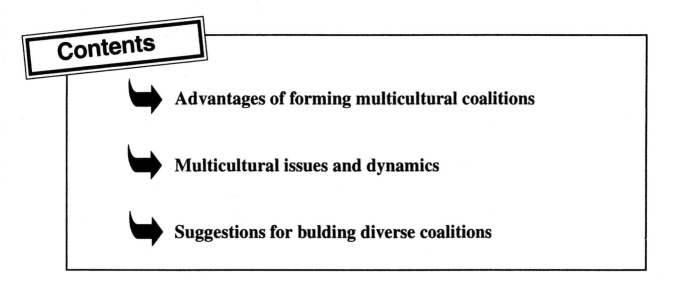

Contents

Introduction

A multicultural organization, according to Jackson and Holvino:

- reflects the contributions and interests of diverse cultural and social groups in its mission, operations, and product or service;
- acts on a commitment to the eradication of social oppression in all forms within the organization;
- is sensitive to the possible violation of the interests of all cultural and social groups whether or not they are represented in the organization, and supports efforts to eliminate all forms of social oppression.

A multicultural coalition is one where diverse social and cultural groups interact to shape the coalition, make decisions, create a unique organizational culture and guide all actions. It defines and redefines itself as a result of the interaction of people with diverse values, perspectives and experiences, and celebrates the contributions of each culture. A collective interest and a culture emerge as a product of this ongoing dynamic interaction.

Coalitions always face the challenge of uniting diverse groups around common goals—the multicultural coalition goes farther, to embrace diversity in each aspect of its work and development, recognizing that the common ground is more than a mixture of its components.

Why Is It Advantageous To Develop Multicultural Coalitions?

Diversity is reality. We are all connected through the increasing globalization of communications and trade, immigration and labor practices; changes in one part of the world affect people everywhere through environmental impact, migration, availability of goods and resources. Within the United States, and particularly in urban communities, people from different backgrounds are living, working, studying and intermarrying together in greater numbers than ever before. According to a Hudson Institute 1987 study entitled *Workforce 2000*, the new entrants to the workforce by the year 2000 will be 85% (5/6) people of color, immigrants and white women, while only 15% will be white men. Our survival is linked with diversity; We need to become comfortable living in such a multicultural society.

It enriches our own experience to work closely with people from different cultures. We learn much from sharing visions, customs, beliefs and values. Exposure to different approaches to problem-solving and social change greatly expands our own vision and contributes new ideas to our repertoire of tools and tactics. Inclusion of varying viewpoints increases creativity and innovation. This is an adaptive response to our increasingly turbulent, interdependent world. Given the increasing diversity of our world and the interconnected problems and solutions we deal with, working together is the best, most viable strategy for accomplishing our goals.

The issues our coalitions work on affect many different groups. All stakeholders have insight into how to address their own problems. By combining perspectives and experiences we can create more comprehensive approaches with much greater impact on social and economic problems.

What Multicultural Issues To Expect In Your Coalition

In multicultural coalitions, we are likely to be working with people of different colors, national origins, ethnic groups, genders, social and economic class, ages, sexual preference, work experience, educational background, spiritual and religious practices and physical and mental ability. Some people may speak a different language, have a different conception of time, interpret events from their unique standpoint. These differences inevitably affect our way of working together.

Few of us have much experience in working closely with people from different backgrounds. Most of our ethnic and racial groups survived by focusing on our own internal development, and operating in insulated communities with uniform norms and beliefs. It is only recently that forming diverse alliances is considered to be practical, let alone essential for our group's self-interest. Consequently, we lack familiarity with diverse behaviors and values, and do not automatically trust each other's motives or commitment.

It is likely that some of us will have experienced different sorts of oppression, based on our identity, beliefs or practices. Or perhaps we are members of dominant groups with privileges which Peggy McIntosh says are "unearned and conferred systematically". Experience as victims or perpetrators of oppression leave us with scars and attitudes that can seriously impede collaboration.

The history or presence of oppression is a fundamental barrier to collective organizing. It may linger as discrimination, or perpetuation of stereotypes or prejudice. But one thing is for certain—it won't disappear unless we actively combat it, within our own organizations and our work with the community. Some types of oppression are:

racism: Racism involves the subordination of people of color by white people. Unlike prejudice or discrimination which are individually-initiated acts, racism, as defined by Delgado is "an institutionalized system which perpetuates both individual acts of discrimination and racial subordination—a system supported by culturally sanctioned beliefs which, regardless of intentions, uphold the advantages of whites."

anti-Semitism: the subordination of Jewish people by gentiles, often leading to violent acts against people based on their Jewish heritage.

sexism: the subordination of women by men.

ageism: discrimination against people based on their age, usually directed against older people or youth.

heterosexism: prejudice and oppression against gays and lesbians based on their sexual orientation; assumption that heterosexism is the only acceptable sexual preference.

nationalism: placing the interests of people from one particular nation over those from other nations.

classism: subordination of people from lower socioeconomic classes by people from upper socioeconomic classes; emphasis on the interests of one social or economic class over those of others; class privilege.

How To Build Effective Multicultural Coalitions

Cultural differences can either enrich or impede coalition functioning. Creating multicultural coalitions challenges us to deal with differences and use them to strengthen our common work. Awareness of sensitive issues and dynamics can help you to detect potential obstacles and develop approaches to address them — either before problems arise, or after they occur.

Building effective multicultural coalitions involves:

•articulating a vision

•conducting strategic outreach and membership development

•setting ground rules that maintain a safe and nurturing atmosphere

•establishing a structure and operating procedures that reinforce equity

•practicing new modes of communication

•creating leadership opportunities for everyone, especially people of color and women

•engaging in activities that are culturally sensitive or which directly fight oppression

Before reading ahead, you might want to have your coalition complete the "Inclusivity Checklist" (Worksheet #1) at the end of this Chapter.

In each of the sections below, typical multicultural dynamics are described, followed by suggestions for addressing or avoiding them.

1. Vision / Context

A. Multicultural Dynamics

history and trust: It will take time and effort to enable groups with historically antagonistic or oppressive relationships to trust each other and begin to work effectively together.

cultural dominance and insensitivity: White people often put people of color in difficult or compromising positions in multicultural coalitions. They may consciously or habitually act superior and condescending; they may approach members with stereotypical notions, or generalize about an entire people based on their experience of one person; they may be overprotective and patronizing, or exclude, ignore or avoid involving them. A frequent complaint from people of color is that when they are in the minority in a coalition, they are asked to teach others about their culture, or explain racism and oppression—rather than having everyone educate themselves or at least approach the learning process as an equal exchange. In coalitions where white people are the majority, people of color may be expected to conform to white standards, to be bicultural and bilingual; this accommodation takes enormous energy to sustain.

The initiating group of a coalition may not be culturally diverse; their reasons for starting the coalition may not appeal to other groups. Their vision may not reflect diverse cultures, issues and concerns. Consequently, some people may not be attracted to it, others may feel excluded or ignored.

B. Suggestions

- Make a commitment to create an organizational culture that embraces and grows from diversity

- Become aware of what dimensions of cultural diversity exist in your coalition

- Respect and celebrate the various ethnic, racial, cultural, gender and other differences in your group. Make the time and create the space for this to occur

- Cultivate a multicultural atmosphere. Incorporate language, art, music, rituals, and ways of working together that derive from diverse cultures. Have appropriate resources and educational materials available, and encourage people to use them

- Provide a nurturing environment where it is safe for members to talk about differences, rather than ignore them

Worksheets #3 and #4 following this Chapter provide opportunities for your coalition to explore "Myths and Stereotypes" and "Assumptions" we make about other cultures.

2. **Membership Recruitment/Outreach**

A. Multicultural Dynamics

membership recruitment: It is difficult for monocultural or homogeneous organizations to cultivate cultural diversity. It usually requires a conscious outreach effort to recruit representatives of other groups. The people targeted may well feel suspicious about the motives for this invitation, the role they will be expected to play, the sincerity of the desire to fully involve them and incorporate their concerns. Entering a coalition with an existing (exclusionary) membership, which has already decided on its goals and activities, is not an attractive proposition. It is even more daunting if you don't know the people or don't trust them.

tokenism: There is increasing pressure on primarily white coalitions to diversify their membership. Some funding sources require it. Also, coalitions lack credibility when working in communities of color, or on issues affecting diverse populations, if they do not have representatives of these groups as visible leaders or members. Recruiting diverse participants as an end in itself — for numbers or visibility alone — is not what we're after. Many problems arise from this sort of tokenism. Often there is no attempt to share power or responsibility; people may be given titles without authority and responsibility without the resources or information to fulfill it — setting them up to seem ineffectual and to look bad.

changing goals, strategies and ways of working: Many coalitions form among people who already know each other, and later realize that they will not have legitimacy or be effective unless they include other groups. In these cases, there is a genuine desire for diversity as vital to the success of the coalition. Becoming multicultural is a challenge, because inclusion of new groups as equal and active members will necessarily change the coalition's goals and strategies, and ways of working. For everyone, especially the newcomers, leaving their place of solidarity and familiarity is a risk that feels scary, and will not be undertaken without some guarantees or trade-offs. Multiculturalism requires moving into a new frontier, defining things collectively, developing mutual trust and accountability based on the recognition of equality.

B. Suggestions

- If possible, include diverse groups at the coalition's inception, rather than later. This can ensure that your coalition's development reflects many perspectives from the very beginning. It can also minimize real or perceived tokenism, paternalism and inequality among the people who join later.

- Consciously give priority to increasing diversity. Consider all the different dimensions of diversity when identifying, selecting and recruiting prospective coalition members.

- Recognize that changing the appearance of your membership - seeing variety—is only the first step toward attaining an understanding of and respect for people of other cultures.

- Welcome and highlight different sorts of contributions, special skills and experiences.

- Provide incentives and trade-offs to recruit diverse participants. Be prepared to operate in new ways, to share control and build trust. Make an ongoing commitment of coalition resources to issues of importance to the diverse group members.

- Respect the right of organizations to maintain their own separatism if they wish. Given their own political perspective or stage of organizational development, they may prefer to strictly work on their own, rather than to join a multicultural coalition. Try to initiate a relationship that might lead to a stronger alliance in the future.

- Develop and use ground rules for your coalition that establish shared norms, reinforce constructive and respectful conduct and protect against damaging behavior (See Worksheet #2 for Sample Ground Rules.)

- Encourage or help people to develop qualities such as patience, empathy, trust, tolerance, and being non-judgmental.

3. Organizational Structure and Operating Procedures

A. Multicultural Dynamics

sharing the work: Different groups will have different degrees of commitment to the coalition's work, and will bring distinct contributions and expertise to the process. Sharing the work does not mean doing everything the same - ideally coalitions need to find ways to value diverse contributions and allow for different levels of participation. Create systems that ensure equity in voice, responsibility and visibility for all groups.

sharing the power: The structure of coalitions often resembles the usual organizational hierarchy, with some group or leader "in charge." This structure creates a power inequity, and is inconsistent with the way that coalition members need to work together as equals, with lateral linkages and mutual accountability.

Respecting Differences

A group of wealthy white volunteers in Winston-Salem initiated an ambitious school reform project for an inner city community of color. They had considerable resources and influence to help improve the school, but did not want to dictate the changes. They formed a partnership with school officials, government representatives and parents of children in those schools. The white women volunteers acknowledged that they had little understanding about the day to day issues faced by the parents and their families, or by the school officials, or government agencies. These players were suspicious of the volunteer group's motives and commitment. The volunteers said, "I want to listen to you and learn how I can help." In a series of meetings, each group described their objectives, priorities and needs. After listening, they began an interchange where everyone suggested approaches and interventions that they thought would help. the cross fertilization of ideas, based on a deeper understanding of the issues from distinct perspectives, led to a number of innovative recommendations which were subsequently implemented by the sustained efforts of this partnership.

B. Suggestions

- Create a decision-making structure in which all cultural groups and genders have a recognized voice, and regularly participate in high level decision-making.

- Make sure that staff and board reflect and represent the community in which you operate.

- Find ways to involve everyone. Use different kinds of meetings, committees, dialogue by phone or mail as means of including everyone in as active a role, or as informed a position as they want. Give people multiple opportunities to participate.

- Make sure that your commitment to multiculturalism translates into the public image of the coalition. When running meetings or presentations, be sure the presenters represent diverse groups — not just as tokens but as substantial participants and leaders

- Structure equal time for different groups to speak at meetings.

- Develop operational policies and programs that confront and challenge racism, sexism and other forms of oppression.

- Conduct criticism/self-criticism of meetings which articulates and builds a common set of expectations, values and operating methods for coalition functioning.

4. Communication

A. Multicultural Dynamics

organizational and personal style: Organizations vary in their degree of formality, comfort with written materials or direct personal contact, concept of priorities or use of time. People need to operate in a manner consistent with their own organization, and to be able to express and validate their indigenous cultural styles.

communication and understanding: Cultural diversity produces differences in interpretation, perspective, assumptions, and ascribed motives. Beyond actual language differences, there are countless nuances of communication that vary by culture, and influence people's points of view. Some people behave more formally in public settings such as meetings; what appears to be objective, professional behavior to them may seem cold or detached to others. Use of physical gestures, tone of voice, and vocabulary may communicate very different things to people from varied cultures. Hugging or handshaking can be a sign of friendship and warmth to some, and absolutely taboo to others; saying no may be the beginning of a negotiation session or the bottom line; establishing eye contact may show sincerity or lack of respect. Coalitions need to pay attention to communication differences so that people are free to express themselves in a way that is comfortable for them, without appearing discourteous or insulting to others.

language differences: Many groups automatically communicate through writing and speaking in English. They do not take into account language differences that make it hard for people to understand information or participate equally in coalition discussions and decision-making. Special efforts to communicate in multiple languages may be required in order to ensure the full participation of a diverse membership.

B. Suggestions

Communication is the basic tool that your coalition can use to unite people from different backgrounds. Communication paves the way for understanding and mutual respect.

- Use inclusive and valuing language, quote diverse sources, readily adapt to differences in communication styles.

- Learn and apply the cultural etiquette of your members.

- Avoid false praise, or other forms of insincere communication.

- Learn to read different nonverbal behaviors, and interpret them as part of the dialogue.

- Make sure that everyone understands words and references that are used. Do not assume common understanding, knowledge of unwritten rules of culture. Spell things out and answer questions so that everyone is up to speed.

- Prohibit disrespectful name-calling and use of stereotypes; respect and use personal names.

- Use humor appropriately—don't laugh at each other, but with each other. If someone makes an insulting joke or comment, the person it was addressed to can say "ouch. " This alerts the group to their discomfort and signals that the joke was not funny, but hurtful. You can further explore with the joker and their target,

"What did that mean for you? What did you feel?"

Another way of handling insulting jokes is to respond as soon as they are said, and encourage the group to say how this joke makes them feel. Never let this slide. At a minimum, take the person aside and alert them to your feelings on the matter.

How To Bridge Language Barriers:

- Accommodating language differences may be time-consuming but it is absolutely essential. Multilingual coalitions should line up bilingual translators or volunteers to help with this.

- Determine whether meetings will be bilingual, or how to use translation. If at least half of the group speaks another language, it is helpful to have total translation of each statement. You may want to break up into small groups, each conducted in a different language, to ensure understanding and participation. The report-back and summary can be translated. If only a few people do not speak English, someone who is bilingual can sit near them and translate or answer their questions as the meeting progresses.

- Encourage participants to raise questions or make statements in their primary language (you can provide translation for the rest of the group)

- If a large contingent speaks another language, they may want to hold their own separate meetings. In this case, make sure that the same agenda and issue are used in the parallel meetings, and request some deliverables—e.g. answers to specific questions, lists of ideas—from both groups, that will connect their separate discussions and move the coalition ahead.

- Make sure that all coalition written materials are produced, read and used in all languages that the group speaks.

- Consciously build a multicultural vocabulary, using terms and phrases that describe cultural relations as they should be. Be prepared for words to change action, and actions to change the coalition in real ways.

Recruitment of Diverse groups as vital to the coalition effort......

ATURA: A neighborhood coalition was trying to develop a multi-block waterfront parcel as a local economic development enterprise for a poor and working class multiracial community in Brooklyn. When they saw that their strategy meetings were attended mainly by white residents, they suspended work for 3 months on their plans, in order to recruit people of color who lived in the area.

5. Leadership Development and Opportunities

A. Multicultural Dynamics

decision-making / power issues: Attention to who is making decisions and who holds power in a coalition is extremely important. Groups with previous alliances or mutual familiarity may assume leadership as an expedient way of getting things done, without considering how this looks to others who are left out of the inner circle. Coalitions should be operated as models of shared power, which means that special efforts need to be made to include all groups and perspectives in the decision-making body.

B. Suggestions

When leadership is shared by diverse people the direction of the coalition is immediately infused with a more inclusive, rich assortment of perspectives and leadership styles. Coalition management is enhanced because the combined experience of the leaders advances awareness of the priorities and requirements for each sector of the membership.

- Develop a variety of leadership positions and a mechanism for leaders to work together, such as a steering committee composed of different committee chairpersons. This enables many people to function as leaders and also encourages an interchange of leadership styles.

- Include different types of people in leadership positions so that your coalition can legitimately articulate a multicultural vision and values.

- Help to cultivate leadership capacity of others, particularly people of color. Help people to gain competence in new areas. Structure in opportunities for shared tasks, mentoring, pairing up leaders with less experienced people so that skills are transferred and confidence increased.

Structuring Diverse Leadership Positions

The Mission Area Coalition in San Francisco created Vice president seats for each of the constituent groups in their membership - e.g. Nicaraguan, Chicano, Chinese-American. This served not only to provide visibly diverse leadership, but to foster greater involvement from each group because they felt ownership of and recognition from the coalition.

6. Activities

A. Multicultural Dynamics

activities that meet everyone's needs: Coalitions may not offer activities that are appealing to all members. Those who join the coalition as a way to create social change need to see action with results. Those who are trying to build community will be more interested in activities that promote cultural sharing and understanding. Some people expect the coalition to produce direct benefits to them or their organization and will be disappointed if the coalition fails to do so. Activities not only need to meet goals, but also continue to build the coalition as a solid group and renew commitment of the members.

social and cultural activities: Coalitions strengthen community by sharing times when work is put aside, and people just get to relax and get to know each other better. Cultural differences are always apparent in choices and details of such events. What is fun for one group may be unpleasant for others, food considered a delicacy for some may be unfamiliar or taboo to others. There may be disagreement about when and where to hold events, what to eat, which activities to organize, whether to invite the whole family, and whether gay couples will feel welcome. Senior citizens may prefer bus trips over disco nights. Some Jewish people don't eat non-kosher food, and Muslims don't touch swine. Not everyone can dance to salsa and meringue music, or understand rappers. Some people like picnics or barbecues more than fancy nightclub events. Coalitions may inadvertently exclude members or supporters because they were not taking their preferences and customs into account.

B. Suggestions

The activities of a multicultural coalition can range from things that support the common good to anti-racism/anti-oppression work that affects conditions in the larger society. Coalitions consciously pursuing diversity must factor in the time and effort to make these happen. These activities should be an integral part of your coalition's work — not a separate set of "diversity" projects.

- Integrate aspects of different cultures into all your activities, rather than holding isolated "multinational dinners" and the like. Virtually all activities lend themselves to a multicultural approach: social events, sports, street fairs, talent shows, campaigns, neighborhood improvement projects, demonstrations and lobbying efforts.

- Consciously develop projects that people from different cultural backgrounds can work on together. Create mixed teams or small groups, so that people gain more experience in working together.

- Sanction the periodic use of monocultural caucuses or teams as a way of valuing the need for each group to solidify its position and fortify its own approach to working with the coalition.

- Conduct special activities to educate everyone about different cultural concerns — e.g. forums, conferences, panels, organized dialogues.

- If your activities are not attracting or involving a diverse crowd, try running special events that are geared specifically to different groups. Such events need to be led and organized by representatives of these groups. Let your coalition or community population determine the issues and events that they feel are important. Don't assume you know what is best.

- Take responsibility for making your coalition's activities and programs address multicultural concerns. Begin with a needs assessment and review of your coalition's track record on cultural sensitivity. Examine any racial incidents, insults, harassment or violence that have plagued the coalition or the community you work in. Remember if and how the coalition responded. Identify strategies or programmatic changes that would strengthen the coalition's multicultural capacity and enhance its response to incidents of oppression.

- Conduct prejudice reduction work such as diversity training or multicultural awareness training to change assumptions and attitudes among your membership or community. Using skilled facilitators/trainers, such training can help your coalition to appreciate differences and understand how to reduce insensitive behavior.

- Network and collaborate with other groups committed to multiculturalism, or those fighting oppression or in other ways promoting social justice.

CONCLUSION

Cultivating multicultural coalitions entails changing the way people think, perceive and communicate. Coalition structure, leadership and activities must reflect multiple perspectives, styles and priorities. Changing the complexion of the coalition is only the first step. True change involves the ongoing process of creating a reality that maximizes and celebrates diversity.

Key Points

- Coalitions are ideal vehicles for building positive multicultural projects and relationships

- There is a difference between recognizing cultural differences and consciously incorporating anti-racist, anti sexist (etc.) work in all aspects of coalition life.

- Coalition leaders need to use strategies and structures that maximize diversity and utilize diversity to increase effectiveness

- Embracing cultural differences is not something apart from the issue-oriented work of a coalition; it is inherently a part of the coalition's perspective on issues, possible solutions, and internal membership and operating procedures.

Resources and References

Agosta, D. and the Women Organizers Video Project. (in press) Women, Organizing and Diversity: Struggling with the Issues. A workbook and video guide to help your organization confront racism, sexism and other oppressions. New York: Education Center for Community Organizing.

Delgado, G. (1992) Anti-Racist Work: An Examination and Assessment of Organizational Activity. Oakland, CA: The Applied Research Center.

Equity Institute Appreciating Diversity Program. (1988) Sticks, Stones, and Stereotypes: Curriculum Resources Guide. Amherst, MA: Equity Institute, Inc.

Jackson, B. and Holvino, E. (1993) Working paper # 11. Program on Conflict Management Alternatives. University of Michigan.

Jackson, B. and Holvino, E. (1988) Multi-Cultural Organizational Development. Program on Conflict Management Alternatives. University of Michigan.

Katz, Judy. 1978. White Awareness Handbook for Anti-Racism Training. Norman, OK: University of Oklahoma Press.

Marignay, Bisola. 1992. Building Multicultural Alliances: A Practical Guide. Hastings Women's Law Journal. 3.2. 245-262.

McIntosh, Peggy. 1990. White Privilege: Unpacking the invisible knapsack. Independent School. Winter, 1990: 111-115.

Panel of Americans, Inc. (1991). No Dissin' Allowed: A training manual on creative approaches to appreciating diversity, reducing prejudice and developing youth leadership. New York: Panel of Americans, Inc.

Simons, George. 1989. Working Together: How to Become More effective in a multicultural organization. Menlo Park, CA: Crisp Publications.

Worksheet #1

Inclusivity Checklist

Instructions:

Use this Inclusivity Checklist to measure how prepared your coalition is for mulitcultural work, and to identify areas for improvement. Place a check mark in the box next to each statement that applies to your group. If you cannot put a check in the box, this may indicate an area for change.

- ❐ the leadership of our coalition is multiracial and multicultural.
- ❐ we make special efforts to cultivate new leaders, particularly women and people of color.
- ❐ our mission, operations and products reflect the contributions of diverse cultural and social groups
- ❐ we are committed to fighting social oppression within the coalition and in our work with the community.
- ❐ members of diverse cultural and social groups are full participants in all aspects of our coalition's work.
- ❐ meetings are not dominated by speakers from any one group.
- ❐ all segments of our community are represented in decision making.
- ❐ there is sensitivity and awareness regarding different religious and cultural holidays, customs, recreational and food preferences.
- ❐ we communicate clearly, and people of different cultures feel comfort able sharing their opinions and participating in meetings.
- ❐ we prohibit the use of stereotypes and prejudicial comments.
- ❐ ethnic, racial and sexual slurs or jokes are not welcome.

Worksheet #2

Sample Ground Rules For Multicultural Coalitions

Instructions:

Many coalitions find it useful to create Ground Rules for group behavior and coalition operation. Agreeing to abide by these ground rules can help coalition members to develop group norms, and design an ideal environment where everyone feels comfortable.

You may create one set of Ground Rules that apply to all coalition meetings, or create special Ground Rules for different occasions. Make sure that all participants have input into creating or approving the Ground Rules, and give each person a copy, or post them on large newsprint in a visible location. Here are some sample Ground Rules that relate specifically to multicultural issues. Use them with your group to create a climate that will work for you. (Your coalition can make up its own ground rules... these are just examples.)

We agree to:

- share information about our groups and learn from others about theirs
- be respectful of the way that others want us to treat them. We will not demean, devalue, or in any way put down people. No making jokes at the expense of others.
- give new voices a chance, and not dominate the discussion.
- combat actively and correct misinformation about the myths and stereotypes about our own groups and other groups.
- keep our discussions here confidential, and respect people's privacy.
- treat our own and other people's ideas and emotions with respect.
- listen and not interrupt while one person speaks at a time.
- not blame, accuse or make generalizations.
- disagree as long as nobody's feelings are hurt.
- treat people as individuals, not as representatives of an entire group.
- respect everyone's uniqueness and our difference. "no 'dissin'" (acting disrespectful.

Worksheet #3

Exploring Myths and Stereotypes

Instructions:

This exercise helps people to practice listening and understanding, and simultaneously deal with the content of some typical stereotypes. It is a useful group-building experience, particularly for people who want to share their ideas about the language of oppression. It requires a group leader/facilitator to provide the directions and help debrief the personal reactions of each pair.

1. Write the following myths on a flip chart or hand them out to everyone.

   - Immigrants take jobs that belong to real Americans
   - Blacks ruin every neighborhood they move into
   - Jews are powerful and control the media
   - Asians are model students and have educational advantages
   - All Latino men are macho and hot-tempered
   - Women belong in the kitchen

   (you can also have the group generate its own list of myths)

2. Have people select a partner from a different ethnic, color or cultural background, or alternatively, the group leader can put people together in pairs.

3. Everyone should select one of the myths and discuss it with their partner.

   - Person A states their position, opinion, or conflict about the myth, while B listens.
   - Person B then restates or summarizes A's position while A listens.
   - Person A corrects and clarifies what B said, until A's original position is accurately portrayed.
   - Then A and B reverse roles.

The facilitator then reconvenes the full group to discuss:

- How does it make us feel to see and hear these statements?
- What is the impact of these kind of myths and stereotypes?
- What have you done/could you do to eliminate this stereotype?
- How does it feel to listen and be listened to?

This exercise was developed by Beth Rosenthal and Susan Lob for the Women's Leadership Development Project.

Worksheet #4

Making Assumptions

Instructions:

While it is sometimes easy for people to make assumptions about each other's experiences, it is much harder to actually try to feel what that person feels - to be in that person's shoes. This exercise if for culture diverse groups who are willing to risk exposing their own assumptions, in order to gain a better awareness of the realities of difference.

1. Divide the group into separate groups according to cultural background.

(or you can vary this by having the group separate by gender/race/class/age/sexual preference or what you like)

2. Ask these groups to answer the following questions, and write their answers on newsprint. Each group has to answer questions as if they were speaking for the other group - making assumptions about what other people would feel and respond.

People of color or immigrants:

- I am a white person in (wherever you are located).
- What is it like? How does it feel?

Whites or people born in the United States:

- I am a person of color/immigrant in (wherever you are located).
- What is it like? How does it feel?

Additional questions for both groups:

- What do I like about being a ______________________?
- What do I find difficult about being a ______________________________?
- What do I never want members other groups to say or do to me?

3. After both groups have written down their answers, bring them back together to compare lists. Ask each group:

- "How accurately did they describe your experiences?"
- "What happens when we make assumptions about each other's experience?"
- "What are the similarities and differences between white and people of color/immigrant experiences?"

Paraphrased from an exercise by the Panel of Americans

Worksheet #5

Breaking The Oppression

> *Instructions:*
>
> *This exercise uses a model created by Augusto Boal, the Brazilian community theater movement leader. It involves the whole group, either as actors or "spectators" - people who are both spectators and potential actors in the skit. This can be a powerful tool for opening up this understanding, as well as discussing the realities of oppression, and options for combating it.*

1. **Set the scene and select actors to play key roles.** Have the group brainstorm situations of oppression that have occurred in your coalition. Choose one to act out. Different people volunteer to take on key roles, including the oppressed and the oppressor.

2. **Act out the situation.** Reproduce the experience exactly as it happened, with detail re: what was done to the "oppressed" and how they responded.

3. **Redo the skit**; but this time, have the victim try to fight the oppression. *(usually this will lead to further oppression)*

4. **Actors change roles and play their opposites.** Victims play the oppressors.

Group discussion:

- What happened in each skit? What are the realities of oppression?
- What was done to increase/decrease the oppression? Was there something the victim could do? What else might have worked?
- What did the actors do that seem realistic? *(often the victim can play the oppressor's role well, but it is hard for others to understand or portray the victim's experience.)*
- Question for the actors: Did playing the other person's role give you any insight into how they operated? How did that affect your behavior?

Adapted from Augusto Boal, Games for Actors and Non-Actors

CHAPTER 6

Dealing With Conflict In Coalitions

by Beth Rosenthal, M.S.

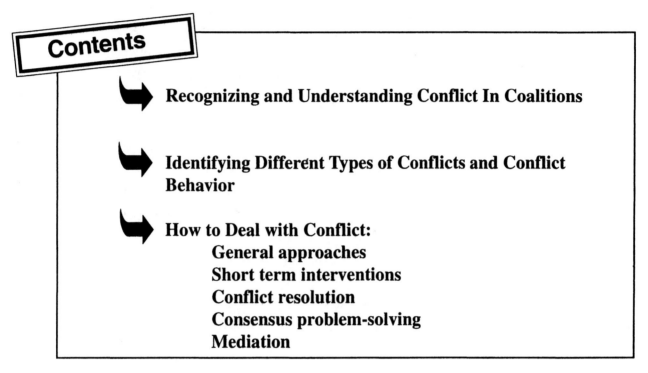

Contents

Introduction

When we work in coalitions we usually expect cooperation and unity. In fact, coalitions are characterized by conflict as well as cooperation. Accepting this and learning to manage internal tension is a central task for coalitions.

Conflict is inherent because coalition participants bring diverse values, organizational styles and cultures, and outcome interests to the process. Sometimes a coalition's members have had problems with each other in the past, or lack trust. Even if groups have collaborated well before, working together is not an easy process, and competition over turf funds, or visibililty is likely to occur. Conflict is also to be expected just because coalitions are dynamic, constantly changing entities. Agreements need to be renegotiated when new members are added, and when circumstances or issues change.

Rather than view conflict as something to be avoided, it is helpful to see that conflict provides an opportunity to examine issues, to learn more about underlying values and assumptions, and to create innovative solutions and programs.

Since conflict is an inevitable dynamic, conflict management is essential for coalition development. Bargaining, trade-offs, negotiating, compromise, and agreement are basic coalition-building strategies. Coalitions really function as mediating structures, balancing differences among their members, and striving, not for unanimity, but for a way in which their members can work together. They seek solutions which can satisfy all parties, and not those where one group benefits at another's expense.

Guidelines For Conflict Management

There are certain guidelines to use in addressing conflict.

1. Preserve the dignity and self-respect of all stakeholders
2. Listen with empathy
3. Disagree with ideas, not with people. Don't accuse or blame. No personal attacks
4. Always define the issue as shared. For example, say "We do not agree about the division of labor" and don't say "John refuses to do his share of the work"
5. Don't polarize the conflicting positions by posing conflict in terms of mutually exclusive positions. For example, say "We need to figure out how to reach the most people in the shortest time" not "Gloria wants to go door to door, and Jose thinks doing a mailing will be better"
6. Allow time to resolve conflicts. If normal meeting discussion doesn't seem sufficient to work out a conflict, set up a special, structured process for dealing with it

Typical Types Of Conflict In Coalitions

Recognizing conflict is the first step toward addressing it. Conflict can occur on several levels within coalitions:

- between the coalition and its members over issues such as expectations and priorities
- between the coalition members themselves around turf, funds, or credit

- between the coalition representatives and their own organizations — around commitments, resource utilization, and authority

Let's take a look at some of the most common conflicts that occur in coalitions.

Power: Ideally, coalitions operate as models of shared power, with all participants involved as equals in decision-making and problem-solving. This is perhaps the most difficult aspect for some members to accept, since organizations are used to acting on their own and making their own decisions. If the coalition includes a mixture of individuals, small grassroots groups, larger nonprofit, government agencies or institutions, differences in power among the participants is immediately apparent. These power differences become sources of conflict if groups with more power expect to have greater control or privileges, refuse to recognize the legitimacy of less powerful members, or resist efforts to equalize power.

In funded coalitions there is frequently a lead agency which, while a member of the coalition, is placed in a more powerful position with responsibility for the program and fiscal compliance of the other subcontractors/ members.

Inequities in power among members may pose operational problems, unless the members develop some form of equalizing power, or accept the legitimacy of different levels and types of power.

Autonomy and Accountability: A coalition must have enough autonomy to take independent action, and enough accountability to its member organizations to maintain the base which is its essence. Conflict may arise if a) the coalition takes action without approval from its member organizations, b) coalition member organizations are unaware of commitments and decisions that their representatives make, or c) the coalition cannot take action because certain members hold up or block the process.

Unity and Diversity: Coalition members share compatible, but not identical, concerns. Coalitions need enough unity to act together and enough diversity to accomplish their goal and to represent a broad base. Coalition functioning requires a constant effort to combine or reconcile differing beliefs and practices. Diversity may be found among coalition members' priorities and ` goals, outcome interests, levels and intensity of commitment, color, class, gender, age, ideology, organizational and personal style, power, and differential contributions. Balancing unity and diversity is the challenge.

Mixed Loyalties: Coalition members are always wearing two hats — one for the joint effort and one for their own organization. It is natural for them to place the needs of their own organization over those of the coalition, but this can cause problems if they abuse coalition resources or contacts. There may be competition for resources, as well as organizational time and energy. Organizations frequently join coalitions for some protection, but participation means assuming a collective risk, because they lose a measure of independence. This tension affects the commitment and contributions that members are willing to make to the coalition, as well as what the coalition can expect from them.

Solutions for power differences:

A government advisory coalition on women's issues was responsive to the concerns of smaller and less powerful groups in their membership. They changed from mainstream policy goals which benefited larger agencies to creation of a new government funding source that gave awards to individual women in less established settings.

Viewing the Coalition as a Means or as a Model:

There also may be conflict between those members who view the coalition as a means to accomplish a specific project or goal, and those who see it as a process for ongoing collaboration. Members who are more goal-oriented want to see action and results, and grow impatient with "process" and discussions about structure and operating procedures. Members committed to the coalition as an end in itself are willing to take the time to build a strong foundation.

Goals and Strategies: Conflicts frequently erupt over goals and strategies. Such conflicts may reflect differences in members' individual goals, needs or priorities; differences about how to approach the same goal; or lack of clarity around goals. Sometimes coalition goals are selected without full input from members, or new members join and have different priorities or approaches. Coalition members may expect everyone to do things their way, instead of recognizing that coalitions have to agree upon goals and methods of implementation.

Division of labor:

Division of labor can also be a source of conflict. Coalitions rarely anticipate or clarify what kind of work is needed in order to accomplish their goals. The role of each participant in the coalition may not be clear, or the coalition may expect more work or commitment from members than members are willing to provide. People who handle a disproportionate amount of the work, or are the only ones to perform the more unglamorous tasks, may become resentful, or feel more ownership in the coalition. The coalition may not be able to finish projects or accomplish goals because the division of labor was not sufficient for the job. Conflict over division of labor is sometimes worse when funding is involved, if each organization does not do what they were contracted to do and the project as a whole is penalized or discredited.

Interpersonal Conflict: In coalitions, as elsewhere, interpersonal conflict may be a problem. Members may have different value systems or professional philosophies that reflect their own personality, organizational culture and style. Some style differences evolve from color, class, and gender, and some, such as personality differences, are purely unique. Coalitions can either accept or attempt to minimize these style differences, and intervene to improve relationships by building mutual understanding.

Underlying Causes Of Conflicts: Regardless of which type of conflict a coalition is experiencing, it is helpful to explore its underlying cause, in order to resolve or manage it. Most conflicts boil down to a few different underlying causes:

- past negative experiences among organizations
- self-interest or hidden agendas
- inaccurate or incomplete information, differential access to information, different perspectives of same information
- poor communication or misunderstandings

Styles of Conflict Behavior

Coalition members may exhibit different types of behavior in conflict: people can approach the situation competitively, attempt to cooperate, while still acknowledging the existence of a conflict, or try to ignore the situation and maintain the status quo. It is helpful to identify your approach to conflict, and to try out other approaches that may be more effective for a given situation. In general, coalitions do best with "win/win" approaches, where everyone is satisfied with the process or solution, rather than "win/lose" approaches to conflict resolution.

WIN/LOSE strategies:

avoiding: Withdraw from the conflict situation or refuse to deal with it. This is most useful when it is best to leave well enough alone, to buy time and when damage caused by confrontation will outweigh benefits.

smoothing: Preserve relationships by emphasizing common interests or areas of agreement, and failing to confront areas of disagreement. Accentuate similarities and downplay differences — this is a win/lose strategy because ultimately one side gives in without exploring all the issues.

accommodation: Let the other person try their solution. This is useful when the issue means more to the other person, when harmony is seen as more important, when you are open to a solution other than your own.

forcing/domination: Force compliance or resist. One side causes the other to acquiesce, gets what it wants at the other's expense. Common mechanisms are yelling, physical force, punishment, sarcasm.

WIN/WIN strategies:

non-resistance - Offer no resistance to the other party's views, blending your efforts with theirs.

coexistence - Jointly establish a basis for both parties to maintain their differences.

decision rule - Jointly set objective rules that determine how differences will be handled. This is win/win if everyone helped to set the original criteria and agreed to abide by it.

bargaining/ negotiating/ compromise: Each side obtains part of what it wants and gives up part. Jointly seek a means to split differences, set trade-offs, or take turns. This approach is used to achieve a temporary settlement, when time is of the essence, when you are working from mutually exclusive goals.

problem-solving/collaboration: Agree to cooperate and attempt to find a solution that will meet the needs of both sides. This approach is useful when concerns are too great to compromise, when solutions affect long range trends, and when decisions will greatly affect all involved.

Creative use of conflict is possible when you are flexible in your approach. Effective coalitions change the style of conflict resolution behavior according to the situation. Worksheet #1 gives your coalition an opportunity to try out these different styles of conflict behavior.

Specific Responses To Conflict

There are several ways for coalitions to deal with conflict: prevention, general approaches, short-term intervention, conflict resolution, consensus problem-solving, or mediation.

PREVENTION

There are many things a coalition can do to prevent conflict before it arises.

participants and motivations: Coalitions need to recognize and acknowledge participants' expertise and treat them as equals. Coalition design should structure different levels for participation, because members will be differentially invested in the coalition's work, and bring distinct contributions to it. Initial planning needs to focus on which stakeholders to recruit, what is in it for them and what would be a problem for them or for the coalition if they joined. People need to be clear about what is expected of them in terms of attendance, participation and commitment, and how benefits or rewards will be distributed. Participants should also have the opportunity to express their expectations about what they want the coalition to do for their group. Using this information, the coalition can provide a variety of incentives to sustain participation, addressing the actual motivations of members.

processes and structure: Coalitions need to establish a multi-layered division of labor, fiscal and program management and accountability. This might be done through coalition agreements, by-laws, subcontracts, and measurable deliverables. Special processes and structures that reinforce mutual accountability can ease problems which are sure to erupt if a hierarchical order is imposed. All participants need clarity regarding how the group will operate in relation to leadership, decision making, allocation of responsibilities and approaches to problem solving. What the coalition can do, in the name of the coalition, needs to be clear to all participants.

Conflicts over exclusion or elitism can be mitigated by developing and using mechanisms for joint **decision-making**. Coalitions can use other participatory planning and decision making processes beyond simple voting, such as nominal group process, consensus, working consensus, organizational vetoes, emphasis on unanimity or dissent. Decision making can be done through use of small task forces which report back to the larger group, through polling of members, through conference phone calls or even teleconferences. The primary task is to give participants the information they need to make informed decisions, incorporate the diversity of ideas and concerns, and move toward consensus.

Conflict resulting from **power struggles** for control of the coalition can be avoided if participants agree on how decisions are made, how they are communicated to the broader membership, how agencies influence the decisions, who is authorized to make decisions, and what is considered binding. If differences in amount and level of power among members is a problem, the following may help to equalize power:

- one group/one vote
- voting/not voting membership
- caucuses for less powerful groups
- an agenda that gives less influential members the advantage
- making powerful groups affiliates or honorary members
- providing technical/advisory status for powerful groups

Autonomy/accountability tensions can be avoided if coalitions clarify in advance what situations will require approval from different levels within the participating organizations, and the process for obtaining this approval in a timely fashion.

When decisions are reached, agreements or even formal negotiated settlements can be constructed and used as needed for reinforcement and clarification.

goals/purposes: Coalition goals and purposes should be clearly articulated and familiar to all participants. It is helpful to explore everyone's perceptions about goals and expected outcomes, because interpretations vary and lead to misunderstandings.

A number of conflicts can be avoided by careful attention to *selection of goals.* Ideally decisions on goals should be made by a broad range of stakeholders, to include a confluence of interests. Some effective approaches include the following:

- Select a goal that is central to everyone's interests and is seen as something that can benefit both the diverse groups and the coalition as a whole.
- Define a goal relevant to the member's interest, but broader than any one group could address alone.
- Identify linkages between the issues. Show how participants' differences support the whole.
- Link short term goals to the long term, big picture.
- Choose a goal that would give something to everyone. Expand or redefine the pie rather than consider possible outcomes in zero-sum terms. Rather than figuring out how to divide the pie, become the pie-maker.

To minimize the dilemma of mixed loyalties:

- Design collective efforts that do not threaten the turf or networks of the member organizations.
- Identify and treat carefully issues or positions that could compromise members' credibility and funding.
- Prevent direct competition between the member organizations and the coalition by agreeing not to interfere with turf, funding or important contacts.
- Be certain that grants given to the coalition are not considered to be substitutes for grants given to individual members.
- Agree on actions that members can do in the name of the coalition and those that they are free to do on their own.

> *Building in Different Levels of Participation*
>
> *•The Illinois Pro-choice Alliance has three tiers of participation for their members, ranging from information-seekers to active lobbyists. People can join at whatever level is comfortable for them.*
>
> *•A statewide policy-making body for the Florida Junior League, composed of over 20 local chapters, built in different levels of sign-off on position papers. Anyone can generate a position on any issue; any member organization can have an ad hoc task force to research issues, and raise them to the full body. Those issues which gain approval by a 2/3 majority of all the local chapters become part of the statewide agenda.*

Conflicts over methods can be avoided by ensuring that the task can be performed by the person assigned to handle it, tasks are well framed, and support provided. Conflicts over **division of labor** can be resolved by dividing up tasks and having everyone share in some part of the work. Approaches include:

- short term work groups
- rotation of jobs
- work days devoted to specific projects
- permanent work groups
- specialization
- use volunteers

General Approaches To Dealing With Conflict

When conflict erupts in a coalition, determine what it is really about. If the conflict is over issues, deal with the issue. If it is personal, try to improve the relationship. Conflicts over values can be managed by attaining some understanding about what each party believes. If the conflict is not being expressed directly, bring it out into the open.

There are several general strategies that can help resolve conflicts:

- using gripe boards, special feedback meetings, or retreats to help people vent feelings, raise questions and clarify issues
- finding areas of agreement and opportunities for cooperation and collaboration
- focusing on common ground and playing down differences
- arranging opportunities for the organizations involved to talk about their differences, remove misunderstandings, exchange information, and build relationships

- helping members to recognize the conflict and to express the reasoning behind conflicting opinions and alternatives
- deciding in advance on criteria for decisions, and using this criteria as a basis for conflict resolution
- discussing acceptable and unacceptable aspects of each position or solution
- breaking down broader conflicts into manageable elements and obtaining agreement incrementally
- working with facilitators or third party mediators who help create a safe environment, provide information, suggest processes for resolving conflicts, make sure each side is really listening to the other, or formally resolve issues themselves

Short Term Interventions

Sometimes you can stop conflict before it escalates. The following techniques can be used to defuse explosive situations.

Defuse arguments: When arguments break out in a group, any or all of the following approaches may be helpful:

- Don't ignore the disagreement. Instead, stop the one-to-one interchange, by rephrasing comments into general questions to the group.
- Ask other group members whether they want to continue the argument or move on.
- Restate the issue being discussed with the hope of clarifying it and taking the focus off the conflicting parties.
- Focus a question toward one of the involved parties, asking for more specific reasons for a particular point of view.
- Ask each of the opponents to summarize the other's point of view. This can help them to see the others person's perspective.
- Ask the rest of the group to comment on the exchange.

Encourage everyone to express anger by describing feelings and consequences, instead of blaming or attacking others. Make comments which are specific and non-judgemental statements about the behavior, your feelings, and the consequences. For example, "When you don't attend meetings, I feel angry because I have to do more than my share of the work." This is less threatening to the listener, and provides an opening to explore how they can improve the situation. Worksheet #1 on "You Messages/I Messages" provides an opening to explore how your coalition can use this technique.

Competition Between Coalition And Its Members Over Funding:
The Northern Manhattan Interagency Council on Community Needs is a community-wide coalition with over 300 organizational members and 14 issue-specific task forces. While largely a volunteer effort, the coalition was desperate for funding for its own staff, office space, mailings, and phone bills. They learned of a special grant that would provide this sort of support for any collaborative effort that involved at least three organizations. Before applying, the Coordinator held open meetings to see which members were also planning to apply, and to present the coalition's position. As a result of the discussion, everyone was willing to compromise. The coalition decided to support all applications from its members and was willing not to apply, if the other applicants could include a portion of their budget to support the coalition. The members saw how they were all competing against each other, and decided not to apply, supporting instead the coalition's proposal, and/or becoming a subcontractor under this proposal. P.S. The coalition got the grant!

Take a Break. Sometimes silence or breathing space helps people to calm down and think of new approaches to the conflict.

Change Chairpersons. Ask someone else to chair the meeting, or help to intervene. A fresh perspective opens up new options, and a new person chairing may produce a change in the behavior of the conflicting parties.

Organize a conflict resolution committee or grievance committee which is prepared to impartially help people resolve their differences through a specific process. As conflicts arise, they can be referred to this committee.

Hold Caucuses. Give the conflicting parties a chance to muster their troops, clarify their positions, and plan their strategy. When the caucuses rejoin the full group, the conflicting parties can intelligently and calmly engage in a dialogue with each other.

The Conflict Resolution Process

If your coalition wants to engage in a full scale conflict resolution process, here is a step-by-step guide. You will need a facilitator or team of conflict resolvers to outline the steps and move the work ahead. The parties to the conflict need to agree to participate in this process, and abide by whatever solutions are reached.

1. Diagnose: Discover what must be accomplished for both parties to feel that their needs are being met. What do they want to get out of the situation? What is their bottom line? Try to sort out the real disagreements from the perceptual disagreements. Be aware of time restrictions affecting the conflict or its resolution.

a. Clarify critical issues: How does each party see the issue? What would it mean to win or lose?

- Define the problem and its cause
- Gather the facts and data that might have a bearing on the problem. Get all sides of the story
- Organize the information and prioritize where possible

b. Identify stakeholders and their approaches to conflict

- What are the characteristics of the parties in conflict — their values, objectives, resources for resolving conflict, approaches to conflict
- Explore their prior relationship to one another, and how this affects their current expectations or concerns.
- How legitimate are the two parties to each other?
- How open and accurate is communication between them?

c. Assess likely sources of disagreement

- Identify and focus on the most important, central issue to the conflict. Where is the most basic point of contention?
- Explore the group environment in which the conflict occurs— the interest others have in the conflict and its outcome. Does the situation promote or discourage conflict?

2. Plan/Strategize:

a. Put together your information on the issues, stakeholders, context and consequences of this conflict. Weigh all the variables.

b. Recognize the conflict behavior used by everyone involved. Decide what kind of conflict behavior is most appropriate. Choose your approach; blend different styles according to your diagnosis of the situation.

c. Practice how you will handle the conflict. Use two friends to practice different interventions/styles. One plays observer, one plays the other party. See if your approach is effective.

3. Implement the Process:

a. Set the tone

- Use group rules to set the tone for the conflict resolution session(s)
- Provide background information, and feedback from your analysis and observations

b. Encourage dialogue

- Actively invite different views
- Help the conflicting parties to air misunderstandings and problem solve

c. Reach agreements

- Use various conflict styles (such as bargaining) to break deadlocks and forge agreements
- Don't impose a solution — help a collective view to emerge from discussion
- Keep testing ideas for group acceptance

d. Document Agreements

- Close the conflict resolution session(s) by documenting the agreement. Write the agreement down, be specific about what should happen and the time that things should be done.
- Decide how results will be monitored

4. **Evaluate Outcomes:**

a. Evaluate the effectiveness of the chosen solution

- Review the agreement and how it is being implemented. Applaud progress and provide support where difficulty is being encountered.
- If agreements are broken, try to find out why. Discuss broken agreements. Was it expecting too much? Was the agreement specific enough? Was the person really willing to change? Is the solution technically feasible? Does the solution have interpersonal or emotional side effects?

b. Follow-up

- If necessary, try another alternative and repeat the process
- Implement corrective or adaptive action if the situation requires it

Worksheet #3 takes your coalition through a Conflict Resolution Drama utilizing skills and concepts discussed in this Chapter.

The Consensus Problem-Solving Process

Consensus problem-solving is a cooperative way of approaching large scale conflicts or issues in which many people must be satisfied with the solution. It takes time — usually several days.

At many junctures, coalitions need to solve problems or make decisions as a group, taking into account different perspectives and wishes. Situations that call for consensus problem-solving are those that affect the coalition as a whole, and require everyone's agreement — for example:

- long term planning decisions
- developing a more effective strategy for social change
- devising a better way to share the coalition's work
- creating a more appropriate structure or leadership role

Conditions That Should Exist Before Problem-Solving

1. The issue or conflict must be perceived/presented as a shared problem. All parties should recognize their common interests and need for cooperation. There should be an understanding that everyone involved is part of the problem and there is no right or wrong perspective.

2. People should know something about the problem-solving process, with its consensus decision-making approach. Make sure they want to go through the process, and agree to abide by the decisions or solutions reached.

3. All participants should enter the process with equal power, information, and support. This process does not work if one party is a scapegoat, or someone holds all the power to influence the outcome.

4. Despite differences of opinion, there should be trust and good faith between the parties. Participants should agree to talk honestly about the problem and take the process seriously.

5. Develop the ground rules, agenda, and process that will be used.

6. Allow enough time to go through the whole process. Do some pre-meeting planning, or start the process by giving participants questions or tasks in advance.

Structure for Mutual Accountability

A university is the lead agency for a federally funded neighborhood drug-prevention coalition. For the first two years, there was tension in the group because of the unequal commitment of the subcontractors, the lack of a common vision for the project, and the need to create a mechanism for accountability to the community. Eventually the community organized an effective Adult Council and Youth Council. Through a few retreats, a new structure was developed which reinforced the mutual accountability of the partners, and created powerful roles for representatives of the community. The whole coalition creates a workplan for the year and determines which partners shall be responsible for each component. A governing body with representation from all stakeholders monitors the project, and the full group, plus outside community members, are involved in its evaluation.

The Process:

1. Hold a series of sessions where all stakeholders can meet together.

2. Agree on what the issue or problem is. Each person should state their needs in relation to the problem, and provide whatever they know about its history and context. Separate thinking about the problem from thinking about solutions. Analyze the problem in as much detail as possible.

3. Brainstorm all possible solutions. Don't judge the ideas. Generate as many ideas as possible.

4. Discuss the ideas, and try to combine them, where possible, to narrow the list. Participants should have an equal chance to voice an opinion before a decision is made. There are a few ways of holding this discussion:

- round robin — each person, in turn, says something about any idea. Each person has a set time to comment without interruption
- pro/con — one person speaks for, and one person speaks against, each idea.
- building unity — one person advocates for an idea. A second person responds to that idea, combining their own opinion and that of the previous speaker. Other people offer their input until ideas are clear and all angles considered. Periodically, a facilitator states the conclusion toward which the group appears to be moving.

If there seems to be general agreement, verify this by asking "do we all agree that ...?" Insist on a response and don't assume that silence means agreement.

If there is no agreement, ask those who disagree to state their objections. Then:

- continue the discussion
- propose a break or period of silence to think
- change the proposal so the objections are taken into account
- postpone the decision
- recess and ask people from opposing sides to work together to come up with a compromise
- take a straw vote to determine how much disagreement there is. If only a few people are blocking consensus, they can let the group override them

5. Plan to put the solution into action. If a decision implies that an action be taken, clarify responsibilities and timetable to ensure that the action is carried out. Hold the participants, themselves, responsible for implementing the solution.

6. Follow up and evaluate solutions.

Now, go to Worksheet #4 for practice in small group problem solving.

Mediation

Mediation involves the use of a neutral third person to help opposing parties to resolve their own conflicts. It is a problem-solving tool for deadlocked interpersonal conflict that prevents people from working together. Mediation is useful when people are willing to negotiate toward some common goal, but feelings of anger, hurt or frustration are interfering with their ability to do their own problem solving. Using a third person as a mediator can open up the impasse.

The mediation process involves discussing the problem openly, airing feelings, and agreeing to specific behavioral changes. The mediator takes the parties through the following steps:

1. Before starting, agree to go through the process and agree about outcomes that you expect.
2. Express all resentments, hurt and anger that distort your communication with each other.
3. Discuss perceptions of the problem. Check out assumptions, expectations, fears.
4. Do a mutual critique of the problem. See how your own actions and behaviors contribute to the situation.

5. Bargain. Ask for what you want. Use this as a starting point, and give the other party a chance to do the same.

6. Listen to what the other party wants. Consider what you can give up or do differently.

7. Make agreements about changes. Develop a written contract or agreement. Promise to work on specific behaviors for a given period of time.

Conclusion

Conflict is an inevitable factor of coalition life. Through creative use of conflict, we can learn more about each other, and arrive at more innovative solutions to common problems. The challenge is to embrace conflict, and expand our ability to manage it.

Key Points

- Conflict is inherent in coalitions.
- It is useful to recognize different types of conflict and conflict behavior.
- Expression and negotiation of conflicts is healthy coalition behavior.
- There are various approaches to prevent, minimize and resolve conflicts.

Resources and References

Auvine, B., Densmore, B., Extrom., Poole, S., Shanklin, M. (1978). A manual for group facilitators. Madison WI: The Center for Conflict Resolution.

Avery, M., Auvine, B., Streibel, B., Weiss, L. (1981) Building united judgement: A handbook for consensus decision making. Madison, WI: The Center for Conflict Resolution.

Brandow, K., McDonnell, J. and Vocations for Social Change. (1981). No Bosses Here! A manual on working collectively and cooperatively. 2nd edition. Boston: Alyson Publications and Vocations for Social Change.

Carpenter, S. (1992). Solving Community Problems by Consensus. Washington, D.C.: Program for Community Problem Solving.

Fisher, R. and Ury, W. (1981). Getting to yes: Negotiating agreement without giving in. Boston, Houghton Mifflin.

Kindler, Herbert S. (1992). Managing disagreement constructively: conflict management in organizations. Los Altos, CA: Crisp Publications.

Mizrahi, T., and Rosenthal, B. (1992). Managing dynamic tensions in social change coalitions. In T. Mizrahi and J. Morrison, (Eds.) Community organization and social administration: Advances, trends, and emerging principles. NY: Haworth Press.

Worksheet #1

You-Messages / I-Messages

Instructions:

Many people use "you-messages" when they are angry about something. A "you-message" criticizes and says that YOU are the cause of the problem - for example, "This place is a mess! You are a slob!" When you send a "you-message" the listener feels attacked, and thinks about self-defense or counterattack which only escalates the problem. Instead of accusing the other person, tell them how you feel about the behavior, your feelings, and the consequences - for example - "When you leave your papers all over the place, I feel angry because I end up doing more than my share of cleaning." This is less threatening to the listener; and provides an opening to explore how they can improve the situation.

The formula for making "I-messages" is as follows: "When you... (unacceptable behavior), I feel... (feeling word), because... (consequences of their behavior)." PRACTICE! This exercise can be used in committee or coalition meetings, or in one-to-one situations. It is helpful to have tow people communicating with each other; and a third to give feedback and ask questions. If other group members are present, they can also reflect what they hear.

1. Form small groups.

2. Think about something that someone is doing that makes you angry.

3. Each person takes a turn to practice communicating your anger, first through "you-messages" and then, through "I-messages." Get feedback from the group. Which message was more effective?

4. State the feeling: I feel...
   State the behavior: when you...
   State the consequences: because...

Worksheet #2

Select the Most Effective Conflict Behavior

Instructions:

This exercise can help you distinguish among different ways of handling conflict. It can be used by individuals, as a way to build your own awareness. It can also be used in groups, as a basis for discussing conflict and arriving at a better understanding of different approaches.

Nine types of conflict behavior discussed in the Chapter are listed below. Once you are clear about what each type of behavior is, answer the questions in the Situations on the following pages. For each situation, write the conflict behavior(s) that you think will be most effective, who should be involved in the situation (the stakeholders), and why you think this approach will work. A tip: there are no really "right answers. Each type of conflict behavior will have different consequences in different situation with different players. Once you choose your answers, discuss or think about the consequences. See if another behavior would result in something different.

CONFLICT BEHAVIOR

1. avoiding
2. smoothing
3. accommodation
4. forcing/domination
5. nonresistance
6. coexistence
7. decision rule
8. bargaining/negotiating
9. problem solving/ collaboration

Worksheet

SITUATIONS:

Your meeting has another half hour to go, and someone has raised an objection tothe last decision made.

conflict behavior ______________________________

participants: ______________________________

rationale: ______________________________

Your coalition membership recruitment drive resulted in 10 new members who want to join the steering committee. The existing steering committee members don't want to give up their power.

conflict behavior ______________________________

participants: ______________________________

rationale: ______________________________

There has been a long lasting conflict in your coalition over tactics. One contingent wants to be more confrontational; another feels that educating legislators about the issue is enough

conflict behavior ______________________________

participants: ______________________________

rationale: ______________________________

Two members of your coalition have never gotten along. If one person says something, the other always disagrees. In a meeting of 30 people, these two members start in with each other again. As the chairperson, you are concerned that they are being too disruptive.

conflict behavior ______________________________

participants: ______________________________

rationale: ______________________________

Worksheet

You have been trying to recruit a certain influential organization to join your coalition. They say that they are interested, but that they will only join if you put their name on the top of the membership list that appears on your publicity brochure.

conflict behavior ______________________________

participants: ______________________________

rationale: ______________________________

Your coalition has a policy of allowing one vote per organization. At your annual membership meeting, all of your member organizations attend, and some of the funded agencies bring up to five staff members who have been active on coalition committees throughout the past year. When it comes time to take a vote, everyone in the room raises their hand. One of the block associations complains that the vote is stacked.

conflict behavior ______________________________

participants: ______________________________

rationale: ______________________________

Your neighborhood improvement coalition has cleaned up a vacant lot. Some of your members want to turn it into a community garden, and others want it to be a parking lot. The tenants who live on all sides of the lot are glad that it is cleaned up, but are concerned about noise and possible drug traffic.

conflict behavior ______________________________

participants: ______________________________

rationale: ______________________________

Worksheet #3

Conflict Resolution Drama

Instructions:

Sometimes it is easier to resolve a conflict by acting it out - taking it out of the real situation and role-playing different approaches. Here is one method. This can be used in a group, with up to five people acting out the situation. A strong facilitator is needed to guide the process, and ask the questions to the audience.

Begin by asking the group to think about a conflict that your coalition has had recently. Set the scene and identify the key stakeholders in this conflict. These will be the roles that are acted out.

1. In a group of at lease 10 people, ask 3 to 5 people to play roles in this skit.

2. Organize a skit portraying a conflict that your coalition is now experiencing. Identify the key characters, the context, and what ever background information is needed. Be sure that at least one actor takes the role of facilitator or mediator.

3. Act out the conflict, and try to resolve it.

4. At any point, people in the audience can stop the action and take the place of one of the actors, or introduce a new element to the situation.

5. Someone outside the skit should debrief the action at each interruption. Ask the group:

    What is going on? How is X feeling, and why? Was it effective when Z did that? Why/why not? Ask the actors how they are feeling in their roles - angry, appeased, etc. When an intervention is effective, be sure to clarify what happened and how it worked.

    Continue to act out the conflict until it is satisfactorily resolved.

Questions that the facilitator can ask the group include:

- What are the critical issues?
- What is each party's stake in this conflict?
- What conflict behavior/style is being used?
- How open and accurate is communication between them?
- Do the parties have any misunderstandings or lack vital information?
- How can this conflict be resolved or managed? List all possible solutions.
- What will the final agreement look like? What will each party have to agree to?

Worksheet #4

Small Group Problem Solving

Instructions:

This exercise presents one way of opening the dialogue about conflict and brainstorming about different approaches to problem-solving.

Begin the exercise in a large, full group, and then break into small groups of at least four people each to have a fuller discussion. Try to mix people in with others they are not close to. One way is to have people count off "1, 2, 3, 4" and have all the "1's" become one group, the "2's" become another, etc. The group facilitator should provide the following questions to each small group. After allowing about half an hour for discussion, reconvene the full group and share answers, listing them on flipcharts.

Have the full group list conflicts that your coalition experiences.

List ways that the coalition traditionally deals with these problems.

In small groups, problem-solve how else you might have handled the situation(s).

Small groups can discuss different options, or even act them out.

Report back on solutions. The group may decide to adopt different approaches in the future.

CHAPTER 7

Involving and Mobilizing The Grassroots

by Gillian Kaye

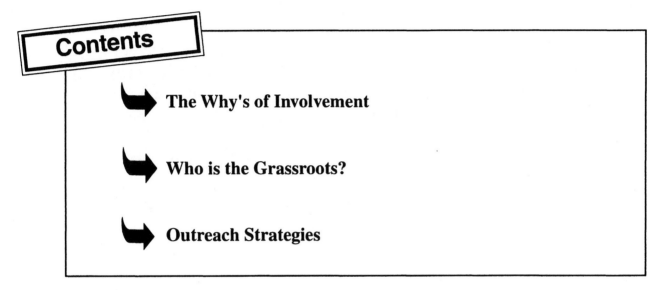

Contents

Introduction

Most of us know how critical it is for the life and effectiveness of our coalitions to involve the grassroots community. What good is it to develop programs targeting communities without residents of those communities helping to shape these programs? We understand that good coalitions cannot rest on service providers and professionals alone.

But often, we feel defeated when we try to reach out and involve the grassroots. We don't understand why no reply comes to our invitations to come to meetings, or when, despite what we feel are our best efforts, we are characterized by grassroots leaders and residents as being unresponsive and non-inclusive.

Perhaps, the fault lies not so much in what we are doing, but in what we are not; and in how we are defining the grassroots in our communities. We need to begin to understand the importance of community ownership, how to create it and examine our coalitions and the avenues we have or have not created for real grassroots participation. Upon examination, the strategies and "how-to's" of involvement and effective outreach begin to show themselves.

Why Will The Grassroots Community Get Involved?

By understanding some of the reasons why grassroots community members will and won't participate in a coalition, you take the first step towards developing strategies to ensure their inclusion. Like any other prospective members of a coalition, grassroots residents expect to play certain roles and have certain power.

Before we examine the "how's" of involvement, we need to do some assessment of why grassroots community members join any given effort. Let's look at three key areas: Coalition structure, community ownership and coalition credibility in the community.

Coalition Structure: The Six "R's" of Participation

These reasons explain why people participate in all kinds of groups, organizations or associations. It has been observed that we are a nation of joiners. Our neighborhood coalitions can be successful when we design organizations that seek to meet the needs of all of our members.

•Recognition

People want to be recognized for their leadership to serve the members of their communities and organizations. We all want to be recognized, initially by the members of our own group and then by members of other groups, for our personal contribution to efforts to build a better quality of life.

TIP: Recognition can be given through awards and dinners, highlighting contributions and praising and naming at public events.

•Respect

Everyone wants respect. By joining in community activities, we seek the respect of our peers. People often find their values, culture or traditions are not respected in the work place or community. People seek recognition and respect for themselves and their values by joining community organizations and coalitions.

TIPS: Don't schedule all of your planning meetings during regular working hours — this may exclude many grassroots leaders who hold other jobs. Meet in the evenings and provide dinner and childcare or at least meet late enough so that those attending can take the time to provide dinner and childcare for their families.

Translate materials and meeting agendas into languages other than English if it's necessary and provide translators at meetings.

•Role

We all need to feel needed. It is a cliche; but it is true. We want to belong to a group which gives us a prominent role, and where our unique contribution can be appreciated. Not everyone searches for the same role. But groups must find a role for everyone if they expect to maintain a membership.

TIP: Grassroots leaders and members have had the experience of being "tokens" on coalitions. Create roles with real power and substance.

•Relationship

Organizations are organized networks of relationships. It is often a personal invitation which convinces us to join an organization. People join organizations for personal reasons to make new friends, and for the public reason to broaden a base of support and/or influence. Organizations draw us into a wider context of community relationships which encourage accountability, mutual support and responsibility.

TIP: Provide real opportunities for networking with other institutions and leaders.

•Reward

Organizations and coalitions attract new members and maintain old members when the rewards of membership outweigh the costs. Of course, not everyone is looking for the same kind of rewards. Identify the public and private rewards which respond to the self interests of members in order to sustain their role in the coalition.

TIP: Schedule social time and interaction into the agenda of the coalition where families can participate. Make sure there is an ongoing way to share resources and information including funding opportunities and access to people in power.

•Results

Nothing works like results! An organization which cannot "deliver the goods" will not continue to attract people and resources.

TIP: To many grassroots leaders and residents, visible projects and activities that directly impact on conditions and issues in their communities are the results they are looking for in return for their participation.

Take a minute to examine how well you have provided for these six "R's" in your own coalition using Worksheet #1

Creating Community Ownership

Now that you have examined your organization and whether or not it is set up to reinforce grassroots participation, let's move on to the next key ingredient for grassroots involvement: ownership.

Creating community ownership requires a change, not only in how our coalition is organized, but in our conception of power and control. While professionals see their job as coming up with the best possible programs and strategies, using the latest research on what works, grassroots community members often experience this as "telling us what's good for us!" Service provider-driven coalitions often prevent community ownership. What are the elements of creating ownership?

First, the grassroots community must be involved in defining the issues. There is no greater "buy out" (the opposite of buy-in) for grassroots community residents than knowing that the coalition has already decided what the issues to be addressed are without the input of the people who are impacted by them every day. When a coalition functions this way, the grassroots community perceives itself as "locked out" and sees the coalition as just another top down model of professional, rather than community, control.

Second, the grassroots community must be involved in defining solutions and strategies. There are no greater architects of solutions than those who are experiencing the problem. The information and skills that practitioners and professionals bring to program and strategy development are invaluable. But the wisdom of the grassroots community, from how to really reach high risk populations to creating community investment to marketing and outreach, needs to be the guiding energy in your strategy development to ensure real success at the community level.

A local community foundation working with a national technical assistance organization helped to begin a coalition in a southern city focusing on the issue of drug abuse and trafficking, mostly in the seven public housing developments scattered throughout the city. Residents in these housing developments had some organization and past history of organizing around issues, but were wary of the effort after dealing with police and housing management corruption; an earlier coalition of service providers also came into their developments for a year with programs and activities and then left when funding was eliminated.

The early members of the new coalition interviewed residents in the development before involving them. They heard about the lack of community involvement in the previous coalition's planning and the anger and disempowerment residents felt.

The new coalition hired a staff organizer whose job was to reach out to residents and involve them in a series of planning meetings in their developments to define the issues, develop strategies and identify the resources they felt they needed to implement them.

Subsequent meetings were also held with law enforcement personnel, service providers and other concerned community actors who were involved in the coalition. This led to a series of final collaborative planning meetings where everyone compared strategies and created a comprehensive action plan that would be driven by the housing development residents with the help of the coalition and staff organizer. All participants felt invested and a great deal of ownership over the plan.

One year later, the coalition had increased its membership and participation in its activities. The residents still run the coalition and are turning around the conditions in their developments.

Third, the grassroots community must know that it will be given tools and resources to control the implementation of programs and strategies. Too often, grassroots community members are invited to our table for planning and then sit and watch as their ideas are implemented by "outsiders" or professionals. Real empowerment comes from the ability to have grassroots community members implement programs and use resources according to their own vision.

For many coalitions, these concepts mean a major shift in focus and the balance of power. Remember that grassroots community residents will be living with the issues and problems we are addressing long after our coalitions are gone. If they come once, don't pat yourselves on the back....they may not come again. But, if you begin to envision these roles as the appropriate ones for the grassroots community, your coalition will be stronger and will see real grassroots involvement.

Build collaborative planning retreats into your coalition's structure where grassroots community members can bring their vision and ideas. Community-driven assessments, which will be discussed in the next Chapter, are another key tool for providing the grassroots with the opportunity to play these roles.

Your Coalition's Credibility

The last link in this chain is the issue of your own coalition's credibility with the community. The history of many coalitions is "here today, gone tomorrow." Programs and resources appeared in communities and disappeared overnight. Promises were made to community residents and never kept, resources promised and never delivered and, as is often the case, residents were never involved in the ownership process and, instead, were delivered services and programs in which the community had no investment or say.

Taking the time to examine and understand the history of coalitions that have gone before yours can be a critical step toward paving the way for grassroots involvement. In addition, the simple step of looking for this information sends a clear and welcome signal to the community that you care about doing it right.

Identifying The Grassroots Community

Before you start developing strategies to involve the grassroots community, it's a good idea to take some time to define who it is you want to and should be involving. This means taking the time to identify real community leadership and to examine what the various "sectors" of the organized and unorganized community are in your coalition's target areas.

Community Leadership

You are probably already working with community leaders. You have the school principal, the Police Chief and several "grassroots" service providers already actively involved in your coalition.

Great! These leaders are important community players and need to be included. But there are other leaders, equally important, that you may have overlooked. The failure to involve key grassroots leaders can make an enormous difference in the effectiveness of your coalition's efforts because grassroots leaders provide 3 of the essential ingredients for outreach to the community: credibility, access, constituency

"Formal" Leaders

Leaders have many qualities. They are people with vision, charisma, commitment and the ability to get things done. Perhaps most importantly, community leaders have a constituency behind them, people who look to them for advice and action.

Identifying "formal" community leadership is easy. Local elected officials, agency heads, service providers and prominent civic leaders can be identified through city and agency directories, local publications and even a trip to the Mayor's office. These leaders certainly have constituencies they can reach out to, access to other leaders in their circle and, with some residents, credibility and clout. These "usual suspects" are easier to reach out to, through phones and faxes and morning meetings.

"Volunteer" Leaders

"Volunteer" leaders are a key group that is often left out of the initial coalition search for leaders. Chances are good that the communities your coalition is targeting have many volunteer neighborhood groups (including block associations, parent associations, merchant associations and neighborhood organizations) that have active memberships. Each of these groups has one or more volunteer leaders.

Not only do these leaders have real grassroots constituencies but they have an access that "formal" leaders do not: to "high risk" and "yet to be reached" populations that may live in their communities. With many community residents, it is these leaders that have the real credibility, more than an elected official who may be seldom seen in the neighborhood or a service provider who lives somewhere else. Grassroots volunteer organizations have many benefits that coalitions need to work effectively in communities.

Finding these leaders can be a bit harder. The first important step is to understand and identify what the potential "organized" sectors of your community might be. We'll do this a little later. Once you have determined these sectors try: reading local community newspapers or bulletins for meeting announcements and events and calling the contact telephone numbers or attending; hitting the streets in particular communities and looking for fliers announcing meetings and events in store windows, supermarkets and pasted up on telephone poles; and checking with elected officials' offices for their community organization listings.

"Informal" Leaders

There are also important "informal" leaders in a community that are essential to seek out. "Informal" leaders fit all of our leadership criteria but may not have a title, a conventional office or even a telephone. They may run or work at a local store, be the adopted "grandmother" of a neighborhood who sits out on her porch or be a drug dealer out on a street corner. As with "volunteer" leaders, these leaders have their own constituencies, unique avenues of access and the highest level of credibility with their own followers.

An active coalition in a small town in Western Massachusetts had come together to work on preventing drug abuse in their community. The first sector of the community they were targeting for their drug and health education programs was the sizable Latino population. A series of public meetings were planned, complete with experts to discuss the issues and give the participants information. Attention was paid to making the meeting place accessible, making transportation available and having childcare so that parents could attend. Fliers were distributed in Spanish all over the town.

But attendance was so low, they decided to investigate and "check in" with a few "informal" leaders in the community. Culturally, they were told, community residents preferred small informal gatherings at someone's home or apartment. Structured agendas were okay, but community members liked conversations better and still always managed to accomplish their tasks.

So the coalition developed a system of small, informal house meetings called "charlas." Here, community residents were "hosted" by another community member at their home. The same written information that had been on hand at the public meeting was available here and residents talked and planned around the same issues using a less formal but still planned agenda.

Over the next few months, a small group of respected women leaders took over the planning and organizing of the "charlas." Now, hundreds of residents are involved in the coalition's work through this program.

Finding these leaders can be accomplished in one way: talking to local residents and "volunteer" leaders. "Informal" leaders are usually well known by reputation, good and bad. Again, the first step to take is to identify the "unorganized" sectors of the communities you are targeting.

Take the time to investigate who the leaders are in your

communities. Without their support and involvement, you are less likely to mobilize and reach the grassroots community, you will have less access to the populations you want to reach with your programs, and you may lose considerable credibility among grassroots community residents.

The "Organized" Sectors of Communities

Every community is different. But each one has a number of different "sectors" or areas that are organized and have credible leadership. The obvious sectors are those which have "formal" leaders such as Voters, Police and Service Providers.

But what about some of the others we have begun to talk about: Neighborhood Organizations, Youth and Parents?

Targeting organized grassroots groups can provide a wealth of benefits for coalitions, including:

1. Community organizations can reach "high risk" and "hard to reach" populations that traditional programs cannot reach through trust, familiarity and history.

3. Community organizations know what works in their communities! This includes the most effective ways to reach people with information and programs, the kinds of meetings and organizations people will attend and join and what will create "investment" for residents and families.

4. Community organizations are community archivists. They know the "history" of past coalition efforts in the community, what has worked and failed and how this will impact on partnership efforts.

5. Community organizations can promote ownership and participation through using their own networks and knowledge.

6. Community organizations know how the community views the CAUSES and SYMPTOMS of problems and the most effective avenues to address them.

7. Community organizations build local leadership that will

remain in the community to carry on the work that is initiated.

8. Community organizations can be more effective in helping to create positive "norms" in the community than outside agencies because of their credibility, locations and ability to reach many populations.

Examples of "Organized" Sectors of the Community

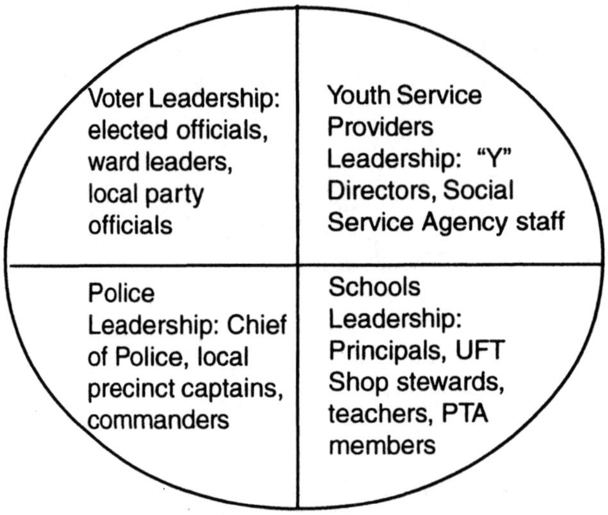

Use Worksheet #2 to identify the organized sectors in your community and its leadership.

The "Unorganized" Sectors of Communities

There are also the "unorganized" sectors of the community which encompass the majority of the grassroots. These include the people who work at the local textile plant, the young people who hang out at the basketball court next to the school, local drug dealers and the majority of parents and other community residents.

As we noted, there are likely strong "informal" leaders present here who you may want to involve along with their constituents. Worksheet #2 can also be used to identify the unorganized sectors of the community as well. Be sure to complete Worksheet #3 which will help you consolidate all of this important information and lay the groundwork for a comprehensive Community Outreach Action Plan.

Outreach Strategies

Reaching out to the grassroots community with your invitation to be partners in planning can be done in a number of ways. While each is effective, when used together, they form a dynamite strategy. Always evaluate the human and material resources you have when considering an outreach strategy but remember: If you stretch yourselves now, the payoff will be well worth it!

Reaching Out to Community Leaders

We discussed the importance of having credible community leadership participate in the coalition. Here are some outreach techniques that work:

• Meet face-to-face with as many community leaders as you can to hear their opinions and gain their insights before extending an invitation to participate in the coalition. Not only will they enlighten you about community issues and perspectives but:

- They'll tell you about other community leaders they know and spread the word that your coalition is worth "checking out."

- They'll identify residents and others you would not have access to who should be involved

- They'll spread the word to their constituency and serve as a great resource for disseminating your coalition's information

• With "volunteer" and "informal" leaders, this may take a bit more time as you build up trust and relationships. Many of these leaders may never have been asked to participate in a coalition before and may have a real distrust of professionals. Go slowly and only promise what you can deliver.

Reaching Out To The Organized and Unorganized Community

There are a variety of techniques that can be used to reach out to both the "organized" and "unorganized" sectors of the community. Whether it is in order to "spread the word" about the work of the coalition, enlist new members for a task force or give the community an opportunity to evaluate programs and strategies before they are implemented, how you reach out is critical.

Public and House Meetings

Town meetings are an excellent way to reach out to the "organized" community. At large meetings, leaders can be acknowledged and praised, you can collect input from community members and strategies and ideas can be discussed. The coalition can get publicity and exposure from these meetings.

The "unorganized" community, however, may not come out as readily to big public meetings. You may want to try the technique of less formal house meetings, held in someone's home, apartment or at a local coffee shop. These meetings have fewer people, usually those who are invited by word of mouth, and have a more intimate and less intimidating feeling. The same things can be accomplished here as at a public meeting but the "climate" is safer and people will speak more freely.

Door to Door

Going door-to-door is a time honored community outreach strategy. It takes time and bodies which your coalition may not have but it can have great paybacks. The advantages of going door-to-door, particularly to publicize a meeting or recruit members are:

- face-to-face contact breaks down barriers and suspicions and always works better

- you are able to get the non-filtered perspectives of community residents

- because you are seen in the community, your credibility goes up and the word goes out on the "pipeline"

Of course there are more drawbacks to door-to-door outreach than just the resources it takes. People are often suspicious to open their doors to strangers and can sometimes react negatively to being pursued at home. In general, however, it's a tactic that works well and is worth the time commitment.

TIPS: Always go in twos, wear identifying insignia and leave people with a flier, brochure or something to remember you by

Street Outreach

If you have decided to reach out to some of the "unorganized" sectors of the community, you have to go where they are. This may mean passing out fliers at factory gates, going out to that basketball court or hanging out on a certain street corner.

Street outreach like this is only really effective when some credible leader or person is doing it with you or on their own.

Tabling

Getting out into the community is really the best way to introduce yourselves. Set up tables in front of busy supermarkets, shops, train stations or anywhere else that people pass by.

Attending Community Meetings

Taking the time to attend local community meetings both as an observer and participant on the agenda sends a signal that you care about what community folks are saying and doing. Never leave your leader interviews without asking when their next meetings are taking place and whether you can attend to observe or talk about the coalition.

Community Driven Assessments

Real community assessments that mobilize and involve grassroots community residents are probably the best outreach tool you can use. The next chapter reviews a process for community assessment. While surveys you mail or use over the telephone are o.k., they only give you information. Surveys don't mobilize grassroots community residents to get involved in all of the key ownership areas we discussed. Rather, they distance the coalition from the actual people that you want to involve.

Now, move on to Worksheet #4 to complete your Community Outreach Action Plan.

Summary Table: Outreach Strategies

1. Reach Out To Community Leaders
•Meet face to face with community leaders to help you: learn about issues, gain access to others, help spread the word and disseminate information about the coalition.

2. Hold Public and House Meetings
•Organize big public or "town" meetings to hear residents' opinions and get your information out. This works best for "organized" sectors of the community and with some community residents.

•Hold house meetings which are smaller and less formal. This works best with members of the "unorganized" community who may not feel comfortable at a big, public meeting.

3. Go "Door to Door"
•If you have the resources, do it! Face to face contact breaks down barriers and suspicions, gives you unfiltered information and will help with your coalition's credibility.

4. Street Outreach
•Go to where the community is, don't expect it to come to you. Street corners, basketball courts, or anywhere else the community is found are all places where you can do outreach.

•Always send "credible" people to reach out — youth to youth, for example. If you can bring a respected leader with you, great!

5. Tabling
•What better way to reach the community than setting up a table with your information in front of a busy supermarket, on a well traveled commercial block, or at community functions.

6. Attend Community Meetings
•Take time to attend meetings both as an observer and as a participant. This sends the signal that you are interested in what the community is saying and doing. Don't just "send someone" — go yourself!

7. Community Driven Assessments
•Implement real community assessments that mobilize and involve grassroots residents. Surveys create distance between the coalition and residents where community assessments that involve meetings and face to face contact can be an effective outreach tool.

Key Points

• Understanding WHY grassroot leaders and residents will become involved with your coalition is the first step towards designing effective participation and outreach strategies to involve them. These WHY'S include looking at: How your coalition is structured, the potential for community ownership and your coalition's credibility in the community.

• Coalitions must take time to identify and understand the different kinds of community leadership that should be involved in coalition planning. "Formal," "volunteer" and "informal" leaders all provide different avenues for gaining three essential things: constituency, access and credibility.

• The grassroots community has both "organized" and "unorganized" sectors. Each provides benefits to a coalition when they are included as a partner.

• Outreach strategies take many different forms. Always assess the human and material resources of your coalition before deciding on an outreach strategy and try to use as many of them together as you can.

Note: The 6 R's were originally developed by Ira Resnick, The Center for Social and Community Development, Rutgers — The State University.

Worksheet #1

Evaluating the "6 R's" of Participation in Your Coalition

All of the following exercises should be done with your entire coalition planning team or any task force or committee that your coalition has whose mission is community outreach and/ or involvement.

Instructions:

- In your teams or as a group, look at each of the "6 R's" of participation listed and, using the worksheet, write down the answers to the following questions

- What do we do now?

- What could we be doing?

- When you have finished, compare your answers as a group. Consider your answers as recommendations for changes your coalition needs to make in its current operations

The "6 R's" of Participation: Group Exercise

1. RECOGNITION:

	What Do We Do Now?	What Could We Be Doing?
a.		
b.		
c.		
d.		
e.		

2. RESPECT:

	What Do We Do Now?	What Could We Be Doing?
a.		
b.		
c.		
d.		
e.		

3. ROLE:

	What Do We Do Now?	What Could We Be Doing?
a.		
b.		
c.		
d.		
e.		

4. RELATIONSHIP:

	What Do We Do Now?	What Could We Do?
a.		
b.		
c.		
d.		
e.		

5. REWARD:

	What Do We Do Now?	What Could We Do?
a.		
b.		
c.		
d.		
e.		

6. RESULTS:

	What Do We Do Now?	What Could We Do?
a.		
b.		
c.		
d.		
e.		

Worksheet #2

Identifying the "Organized" and "Unorganized" Sectors of the Community

Instructions:

• *Label each of the wheels, one "Organized" and the other "Unorganized." Brainstorm all of the possible sectors in each wheel. You can redraw the wheels on large flip chart paper and hang it in the front of the room.*

• *When you have finished, turn to the Worksheet #3. Follow the instructions.*

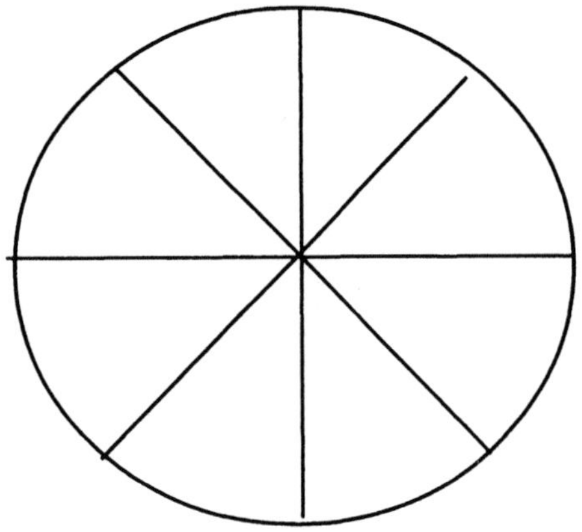

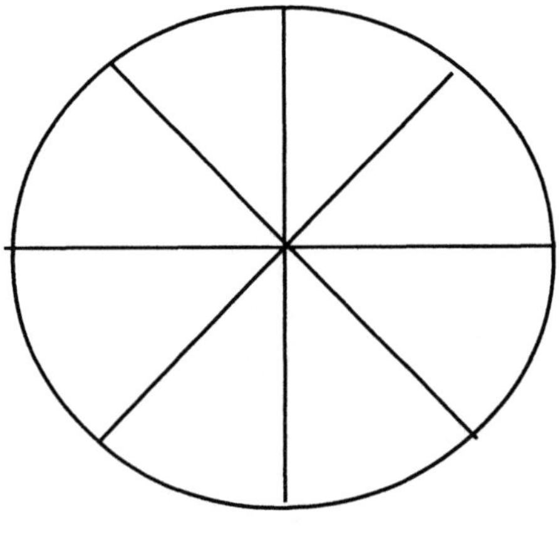

Worksheet #3

Community Outreach Tool I

Instructions:

After you have completed identifying the various sectors of the community your coalition wants to target, you need to begin to locate the leaders you'll be reaching out to and begin to "take stock" of the resources you have and need to reach out effectively.

- *Transfer the community organization and institution from the "Organized Community" wheel that you completed in the previous worksheet. Next to each one, list the leader (or leaders) of these organizations that your coalition members have identified. Add as many lines as you need to include all of the important groups.*
- *When you have completed the exercise for the "Organized Community," do the same for the "Unorganized Community."*
- *Last, brainstorm the resources you might need to do your outreach. Consider person-hours, money for fliers, hiring young people to help with outreach and refreshments for "charlas."*

Target Community____

Organized Community

1. Organizations/Institutions: Leaders:

Organizations/Institutions	Leaders
______________________	______________________
______________________	______________________
______________________	______________________
______________________	______________________

Worksheet

Unorganized Community

2. Sectors/Groups:

Leaders:

3. Resources needed:

Worksheet #4

Community Outreach Planning Tool II

Instructions:

The worksheet on the next page will help you organize all of the information you have collected for reaching out to the "organized" and "unorganized" sectors of the community.

- *Using the information from the Community Outreach Planning Tool I, follow the columns on this worksheet. List each leader, the method of outreach you would use to contact and involve them, who* SPECIFICALLY *from your coalition or the community "at-large" needs to work with you, the timeframe and any additional resource you need to collect before you begin.*

  REMEMBER: "resources" can be people, money, time, locations, advertising, just about anything!

- *Feel free to make copies of this worksheet if you have more information than will fit on one page. You should be aiming to create as comprehensive an outreach plan as possible.*

- *When you have finished, make sure: (a) the plan is presented to the coalition (or task force) for approval and (b) anyone who you have listed as a "helper" has been contacted and has agreed to participate.*

Community Outreach Planning Tool

Target Community:____

Organization/Leader	Outreach Method	Who's Helping	Resources Needed

CHAPTER 8

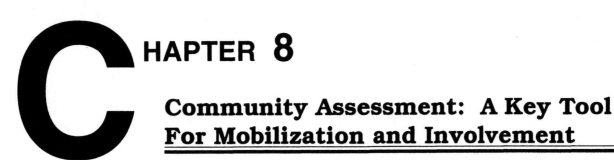

Community Assessment: A Key Tool For Mobilization and Involvement

by Gillian Kaye & David Chavis

Contents

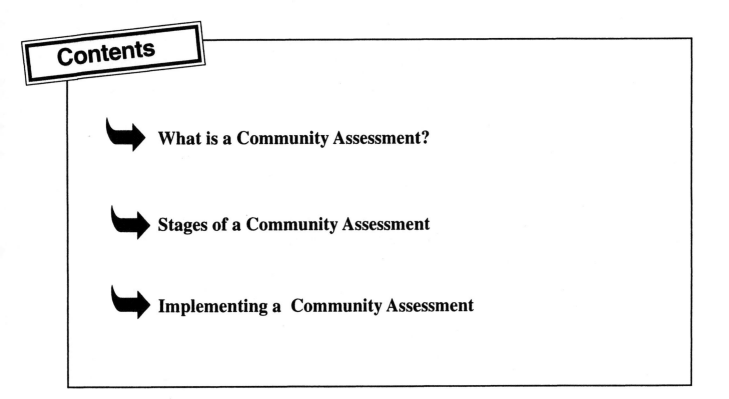

What is a Community Assessment?

In the previous chapter, creating grassroots community ownership and involvement were discussed as key components of an effective coalition effort. Ownership comes from being an integral part of defining issues and solutions and being a real, not token, part of coalition planning from beginning to end.

Community assessment is a mobilizing process where all of the key sectors of the "organized" and "unorganized" community can play these important planning roles. Through this process of meetings, planning sessions and information sharing the coalition can:

- develop community ownership of issues and solutions
- gain information about needs and resources in a community
- identify opportunities and barriers

♦ begin to mobilize the key sectors of the community to take action

How Does a Community Assessment Work?

An effective community assessment is done with all of the key sectors of a given community. Key sectors are all of the areas of your community that can and should give input into the coalition's planning process. It can be done in multiple communities at the same time or one after another. Fundamentally, it is a week of identical meetings and planning sessions facilitated by community members and targeted to each "sector" of the community. The assessment ends with follow-up and feedback to the community and clear invitations for the community to become involved in the coalition's planning.

Community assessment consists of six components, all administered by a ***core planning group*** of leaders or their delegates representing the sectors your assessment will target. The core planning group decides on the objectives for the assessment, which community sectors to target, outreach strategies and meeting schedules and is responsible for implementing the assessment (including facilitating meetings) and collecting all of the data and information that it yields.

The six components of the community assessment are:

- Community meetings
- Focus groups
- A "briefing book"
- Citizen surveys
- A resource inventory
- Coalition expansion

Each component of the community assessment creates greater grassroots involvement in your coalition through information sharing, collaborative planning, outreach and feedback to the community.

Along with increased community ownership and expansion of your coalition to include real community participation, the community assessment process yields some significant concrete results:

- A "briefing book" containing important archival data on the target communities

- Recommendations for activities, strategies and programs
- Transfer of training and other skills to community leaders and members.

Don't panic! You don't have to remember all of the information in this chapter to implement a successful community assessment. A complete set of facilitation handouts and training tools follows in the Worksheets of this chapter.

STAGES OF A COMMUNITY ASSESSMENT

Organizing the Core Planning Group

Because they will be responsible for implementing the process, your first step is to assemble your core planning group.

The core planning group should be reflective of all of the community "sectors" you will want to target with your assessment. Members of the core planning team can be leaders that you have reached out to or representatives from these community "sectors" that leaders have recommended.

The important thing is that each member can commit a good portion of their time over the next week or two to the assessment process.

The core planning group, as we stated earlier, will have significant responsibility for the initial implementation phase of the community assessment. Specifically, they will be responsible for:

Deciding On The Objectives and Community Sectors To Target. The community assessment targets organizations and their leaders within each sector and invites them to "host" a community meeting or focus group that will be facilitated by one of the community planning group members. Because your planning group members represent many of these sectors, it is their task to identify any sectors who are missing and which institutions to target. For example, the local minister from the interfaith council hosts a meeting at her church.

Scheduling Meetings and Issuing Invitations. Invitations to community leaders and organizations to host community planning meetings will occur through person-to-person contact between the planning group member and the local leader/host, formal invitation letters and follow-up phone calls. The community planning group members will also have to decide on meeting sites, who to invite to the meetings and the type of meeting that should be organized.

Facilitating and Assisting at Community Meetings. One of the key elements of the community assessment is that each meeting that is held follows an identical format and agenda. This will be discussed in greater detail a little further into the chapter. Community planning group members will play many different roles at these meetings, the most important of which is running the meeting through facilitation.

Collecting Meeting Data. The goals of the community meetings are to create community involvement and mobilization and to gain valuable advice and input from meeting participants. Community planning group members will be responsible for assembling and cataloguing this information for its eventual inclusion into "reports" that will be returned to the community for feedback.

IMPLEMENTING A COMMUNITY ASSESSMENT

Once the initial preparation stages have been done by both the community planning group and the coalition, you are ready to implement your community assessment. Although the process is a detailed one, each step is designed to maximize community participation and ownership.

Community Meetings

How Many Community Meetings Should We Plan?

The most important thing about the community meetings is that there is at least one for each targeted sector of the community. Generally, community meetings in the assessment process run best when there are no more than 10 participants, so the number may vary depending on the response your invitations to leaders and organizations receives.

Schedule as many meetings as possible to fit into a five day period, allowing for logistics such as travel to the different parts of a community or different communities altogether. The last meeting of the day should end by 4:00 p.m., so that there will be time for processing the day's information and to plan for the next day.

On Fridays, activities should end around noon. There will be a need to schedule 1 or 2 evening meetings to interview community leaders and residents who are unable to take off from work to attend day sessions.

How Are Community Assessment Meetings Run?

All community meetings are conducted by a community planning group "facilitator" who is a member of that community sector or institution. In addition, another member of the planning group acts as a "recorder"and records all of the participants' comments on large newsprint in the front of the room.

The meeting is a carefully planned discussion designed to collect input from the participants. The same agenda is followed at all of the community meetings so that each group is sharing identical information. The discussion is guided by the following agenda:

1. Introductions
2. Review of Agenda and Ground Rules
3. Problems and Issues
4. History
5. Strengths and Resources
6. Barriers and Challenges
7. Advice
8. Concerns and Other Topics

A more detailed explanation of each agenda item and its importance is included in the Worksheets section of this chapter.

Who Can We Ask To Be Involved?

Identification and recruitment of participants is very important. People will attend the community meetings and get involved in the assessment process for many reasons:

- The community and its issues are important to them
- They believe they have something to contribute
- They expect that something positive will come from their

effort

•They have a vision of a better community and values that support that vision

Participants at the community meetings should have: knowledge and interest/concern, something identifiable in common, diverse qualities and characteristics (age, race, gender, interest, skills and/or a mix of roles and responsibilities within an organization), and a willingness to be involved in the process.

How Does the Community Planning Group Recruit Participants?

First, the community planning group members should target individuals in organizations within the community that already exist. This includes neighborhood associations, church committees, day care centers and churches.

Try to recruit as many people as possible. Approach each person, if you can, and ask them to attend the community meeting on the date that has been set. Personal invitations usually work better than a letter! Explain why you want them to be involved, the purpose of the meeting and the location.

Remember, if you are targeting a school, make sure you hold several meetings; one each for parents, teachers and staff and students. For targeting churches and other places of worship, ask members you know to recruit from organizations within the institution.

It is often easier to recruit friends and others we know, but sometimes it is easier to invite strangers to participate. Think of ways you can get as many people as possible involved! Make sure to keep a list of names, phone numbers and addresses as you build your participant "inventory."

What Materials are Needed For the Meeting?

Each meeting will need the following materials:

- Name tags
- Sign-in sheets for participants (name, address and phone number)
- Easels (two if possible)
- Newsprint
- Masking Tape

- Markers (a few colors)
- Agenda for the Meeting

You may want to tape-record or videotape your meetings. That's fine but you must always ask the whole group if this is okay. If someone says no, you probably shouldn't continue. This breaks trust and may disinvest other participants.

What is the Role of the Facilitator At the Meeting?

A facilitator is a resource person and leader, not someone with all the answers. Her role is very important in the community meetings. She will be responsible, not only for moving the process along and helping the group accomplish its objectives, but for creating a meeting climate that is safe for everyone to participate.

Facilitators are non-judgmental and supportive. They provide only essential information but never opinions. In addition, a facilitator's role includes:

- giving clear instructions and guidance about activities
- monitoring the meeting to keep on time but allowing for extra discussion when needed

One of the biggest jobs for a facilitator is to see that participants stick to meeting **Ground Rules.** Ground rules help to keep the group in order and make participants feel comfortable and safe to discuss ideas.

Post the ground rules on newsprint in the front of the room. If people do not keep to them, politely mention that the guidelines are to be followed and keep the meeting on task. Always get the group's agreement on the ground rules before moving to the meeting's agenda.

What Are the Other Roles For Community Planning Group Members at the Meeting?

While one member is facilitating and another recording, other members can participate by taking on one of the following roles:

- Welcoming people as they arrive
- Introducing people to each other

- Serving refreshments
- Keeping track of people signing in on the sign-in sheet
- Handling last minute logistics problems
- Helping with transportation if people need assistance getting to and from the meeting

How Do We Collect Information From Newsprint?

During the meeting, be sure that the recorder uses clear printing and the words of the participants. This is critical for creating investment. The recorder or facilitator can condense or summarize what the person has said but should be sure to "check back" with the person for accuracy by asking "Is that what you mean?"

When the meeting is over, take the time to go over the newsprint to check for abbreviations and fill in or add information that will help explain each item in detail. Remember, many of the people who will be working with this information later will not have been at the meeting!

Label the newsprint with the name of the facilitator and recorder in case there are questions later. Be as clear as you can.

Complete facilitator guidelines are included in the Worksheet section of this Chapter. They will provide the tools that the coalition community assessment facilitator needs to train community planning group members and provide important pointers for conducting community assessment meetings.

Tasks for the Coalition

While the community planning group is working on its activities and tasks, your coalition will have some critical tasks of its own.

Selecting a "Facilitator" and Training Community Planning Team Members. The coalition needs to assign someone the task of coordinating the community assessment process. This person will also be responsible for training the community planning group members in how to facilitate the community meetings and the additional tasks they are responsible for during the process.

Developing the "Briefing Book." Additional archival data should be collected on the communities you are targeting in your assessment and compiled into the "briefing book." This book will be used later to give to community members and to support and compliment the recommendations that emerge from your community meetings. Data can include crime statistics, health and disease information, demographics and other relevant information that forms a "picture" of the community.

Creating a "Kick-off" Event. Your coalition should create attention and recognition for this great community-wide mobilization and planning effort. A "kick-off" event to announce the beginning of the community assessment will gain wider recognition for the coalition in the target communities and create a feeling of excitement and expectation. The event can be a ceremony with the Governor or other important elected officials, a symbolic ribbon-cutting ceremony at the first planned community meeting site hosted by community leaders or anything else that you feel will generate publicity.

Be sure to pay attention to generating press coverage. You want as many people as possible to know the community assessment is beginning and that you have begun this intensive effort to fully involve the community in your coalition.

Compiling the "Reports," "Executive Summaries," and "Recommendations." Although the community planning group members will deliver the data from the meetings, it is up to your coalition members to compile this information, **in conjunction with the community planning group**, into three documents that will be accessible to and delivered back to the communities you have targeted. **"Reports"** are a compilation of **all** of the meeting summaries and "briefing book" information from that particular community. **"Executive summaries"** are the meeting summaries and the **"Recommendations"** of the coalition for action steps based on the meeting information. In addition, the executive summaries should include any particular "briefing book" information that supports these recommendations.

Organizing "Feedback" to the Community. When the reports, summaries and recommendations have been compiled and developed, they need to be returned to the community for feedback and adjustments. This will be done either through mailing of the executive summaries, convening a special series of "feedback" meetings or a combination of both approaches.

Recruiting New Coalition Members and Expanding the Coalition. During the community assessment process, members of the community planning group and many of the meeting participants will prove to be important new recruits for the coalition. Strategies need to be developed to enlist them in the coalition either through task forces and committees or asking them to sit on the coalition's board of directors or main planning body.

To summarize, the seven stages of the community assessment are:

1. The community planning team meets with the community assessment facilitator and is trained in the process.

2. Community meetings are held throughout the local area during a one week period.

3. Feedback from the meetings is brought back to the coalition and the community planning group for analysis of findings.

4. The community planning group and the coalition develop recommendations around each major priority area.

5. Feedback is given to the community at large.

6. Relationships are formalized and collaborations are explored with community groups.

7. Plans and recommendations are brought to an action planning session, implemented and evaluated.

COLLECTING THE INFORMATION AND FEEDBACK

What Happens to the Newsprint Data?

When all of the meetings are finished and the newsprint sheets have been collected, it is time to create summaries for each meeting.

As we discussed earlier, these summaries will be included in the feedback "reports" distributed to the meeting participants.

Designate a group of members from your coalition to work with the community planning group for this activity. Don't let the work fall only on the shoulders of your community partners. The participant responses to the "advice" portion of the agenda may include some concrete recommendations for action, strategies or programs. These should be summarized under a heading of "recommendations."

How Do We Get Feedback From Participants?

The "reports" that you develop, containing the meeting summaries, "briefing book" information and "recommendations" must now be shared with participants for feedback and adjustment. This step is a critical one for closing the circle of community ownership and investment.

The "reports" should be mailed to participants as quickly as possible after the week of meetings has ended. There are two ways you can solicit feedback from meeting participants: asking for their written feedback or convening a series of special meetings to get verbal reactions.

If you have the time and resources, holding one more round of meetings is the best option. At a meeting, participants can respond to the process of the community assessment as well as the contents of the "reports" and the coalition members will be afforded the opportunity to meet more concerned community residents who are potential coalition recruits.

Of course, people may be "meetinged out" by this point in the process! Check in with your community planning group about what they think is the appropriate and best way to conduct the feedback portion of the assessment process.

Tying it All Together: Action Planning

The community assessment process has yielded a wealth of information for the coalition to use to guide its strategy and program development. In addition, you have created an enormous amount of community investment and recruited a number of new community leaders and members on to your coalition's committees, task forces and planning bodies.

Now, you will move on to the next and maybe most exciting phase of your coalition's work: Creating action plans for identifying and implementing your final program.

Note: The Community Assessment Process was originally developed by Michael Felix, Paul Florin and David Chavis.

Key Points

- Community Assessment is a mobilizing process of meetings, planning and information sharing where your coalition can: develop community ownership, gain information about needs and resources, identify opportunities and barriers and begin to mobilize key sectors of the community to take action.

- A core planning group of community leaders administers the Community Assessment process including deciding what sectors of the community to target, facilitating action planning meetings and collecting data to deliver back to the community.

- The heart of the Community Assessment is community meetings attended by representatives from all of the sectors of the community. The agenda for the meetings gives participants an opportunity to discuss community problems and issues, history, strengths and resources, barriers and give advice to the coalition about future directions.

- The Community Assessment process yields a wealth of information for the coalition to use to guide its strategies and planning, creates community investment and recruits new community leaders to be members of your coalition's committees, task forces and planning bodies.

Worksheet #1

How the Leader Runs the Community Assessment Meeting

Instructions:

What follows is a leader's guide to implementing Community Assessment meetings. It should be used by members of the Core Planning Team and other leaders they recruit to facilitate Community Assessment meetings. The last page is a check list of tasks for the coalition members to use when implementing a Community Assessment.

The meeting is conducted by a "leader" who recruits between 10-15 people to attend the meeting. The participants respond to a list of planned questions designed to collect input from people.

What is my role as Leader?

The role of **Leader** is very important.

The **Leader**:
- Recruits 10-15 people to attend the meeting
- Encourages everyone to contribute their views
- Asks the questions on the **Agenda**
- Sticks to the **Agenda** and **Ground Rules**
- Gives clear instructions
- Stays non-judgemental

The meeting usually will last about 1 1/2 hours.

The Leader displays the Agenda and the Ground Rules in the front of the room so all the participants can see them. (You may use the pages included here).

Ground rules are important to the success of every meeting. Write them out on newsprint and display them at each meeting. Your biggest job is seeing that the rules are kept and people feel comfortable and safe to discuss ideas. Encourage all people to contribute. If some people seem quiet, ask for their input, but do not push.

The Leader explains that if people don't keep the ground rules, the Leader will politely mention that the guidelines are to be followed and keep the meeting on task.

Worksheet #2

Ground Rules for Meetings

- **Contribute ideas and participation**
- **Stay on task/agenda**
- **Listen to and respect others**
- **You have a right to disagree, but no put-downs**
- **Try to reach consensus**
- **Begin and end on time**

Bin Topics: *Sometimes issues that are very important to participants will be a topic of discussion. If the topics do not fit your agenda or the section of the meeting, write that topic on a separate newsprint titled "Concerns and Other Topics." It is important to collect these as concerns and discuss them later if appropriate.*

Worksheet #3

How The "Recorder" Helps To Run The Community Assessment Meeting

The comments made at the meeting are recorded on newsprint or a large sheet of paper. The person who does this is called the "Recorder."

What is my role as a "Recorder"?

The role of the **Recorder** is very important.

The **Recorder**:

- Keeps the official record of the meeting
- Writes down the main comments made by the participants
- Makes sure to collect the sign-up sheet to keep the record of who attended the meeting
- Records the answers to the questions on the Agenda
- Keeps the list of the Top Three (3) Priorities and the list of the Two (2) Leaders selected by the group

Discussion Guide for Leaders: Community Assessment Meeting

This brief discussion guide may help to facilitate the discussion in your Community Assessment meeting. It offers some questions to help you to collect the input from the participants and to follow the agenda.

I. Introductions (5-10 minutes)

A. Welcome participants and introduce yourself
B. Explain who's been involved:
- Partnership for Families and Neighborhoods
- Support from your church, school or organization

C. Explain purpose of the meeting
1. To conduct a community assessment
2. To identify issues and needs
3. To identify resources and obstacles
4. To mobilize the community

D. Ask participants to introduce themselves (name, why interested, where they live, or other things that will help the group get to know each other)

II. Agenda and Ground Rules (5 minutes)

A. Explain Ground Rules and display them so all can read:

1. Contribute ideas and participate
2. Stay on task/Agenda
3. Listen and respect others
4. Right to disagree, but no put-downs
5. Begin and end on time.

B. Explain Bin Topics (*Items not on agenda that will be listed on newsprint for later discussion.*)

III. Problems and Issues (15 minutes)

A. Explain the types of issues you are seeking. Give some examples.
B. Ask Recorder to list issues on newsprint
C. Ask the group:
1. ***What issues do you face in this neighborhood?***
a) ***What specific instances can you identify?***
Or, ***Can you give me an example?***
Or, ***Who's affected by this problem? Where does it happen? When?***
b) Listen to each individual; summarize and restate so each item is clear.
c) Respect everyone's input; make sure the **Ground Rules** are followed.
d) Ask: ***Do others experience this as an issue too?***
e) Ask: ***Any other issues?*** Generate as many issues as you can.

2. Prioritize the list, generating the **Top Three (3) Priority Issues:**
a) Review the list
b) Combine duplicate issues with group's input
c) For each item, ask people to vote: ***How many would say that this is one of the major issues facing your neighborhood?***
d) Record votes next to each issue (**Recorder** can help with counting)
e) Select the **Top Three (3) Priority Issues:** Identify, based on voting, the **Top Three (3) Priority Issues** facing the neighborhood

IV. History of Solving These Issues (15 minutes)

A. Ask **Recorder** to list all History responses on newsprint
B. Ask the group:
1. ***When has this community come together to solve these types of iss***ues?
2. ***When have different groups or different segments of the community worked together?***
3. ***Which groups or coalitions are working to address these issues?***
C. Review list. Ask, Any others? (If there are efforts by single organizations, list them under **"Strengths and Resources"** in the next section)

V. Strengths and Resources (15 minutes)

A. Ask the group to discuss next the strengths and resources available to help the families and neighborhoods to solve their shared problems and issues.
B. Ask the **Recorder** to list all the **Strengths and Resources** on newsprint.
C. Ask the group:
1. ***What types of Strengths and Resources can be used to support a better neighborhood?***
2. ***What are some of the Strengths of our community or our neighborhood?***
3. ***What Resources exist in our community that can be used to solve these issues?***

VI. Barriers and Obstacles (15 minutes)

A. Ask the group, ***What barriers keep the neighborhood or community from solving issues and meeting the needs of the community?***
B. Ask the group:
1. ***What barriers keep us from solving issues?***
2. ***What else keeps the community from solving these issues?***
3. ***Are there any changes expected that could create an obstacle?***
C. Review the list. Discuss reactions to **"Barriers and Obstacles."**

VII. Set Top Three Priority Issues

A. Look at the list of **Problems and Issues**
B. Ask the group to combine the issues which relate to one another.
C. Each member of the group votes three (3) times, selecting the three issues they consider most important.
D. Add the number of votes received by each issue. The three issues which received the greatest number of votes are identified as the **Top Three (3) Priority Issues** facing the neighborhood.

VIII. Select Two Leaders

A. Select **Two (2) Leaders** to represent the group to the steering committee. As was done with the priority issues, this may be done through voting.

Worksheet #5

Checklist For Community Mobilization Week

TASK	WHO	BY WHEN
1. Decide on the team		
2. Scheduling/Invitations		
a. Decide on sites, who to invite, and types of meetings		
b. Develop list of invitees		
c. Identify local hosts		
d. Develop letters		
e. Send letters		
f. Follow-up phone calls		
3. Briefing Book for Core Planning Group		
4. Household Survey (if used)		
a. Develop Questionnaire		
b. Develop Sampling Plan		
c. Implementation		
d. Analyze and Report		
5. Executive Summaries		
a. Typing and Duplication		
b. Mailing		
c. Receiving and Compiling Feedback		
6. Reception/Opening Event		
7. Publicity		
a. Newspaper, newsletters		
b. TV		
c. Radio		

Worksheet

	WHO	BY WHEN
8. Report a. Coordinating and Editing b. Writing of Outline c. Writing of Sections d. Review e. Publishing and Distributing 9. Planning Next Steps		

CHAPTER 9

Developing Action Plans For Your Community Coalition

by Gillian Kaye

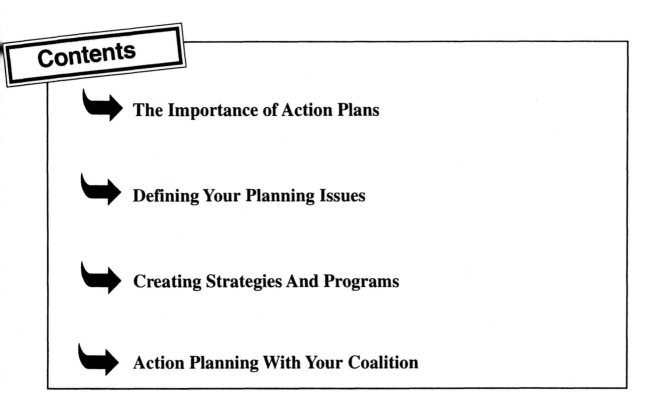

Contents

Introduction

The goals and objectives for your coalition have been set. You have done your outreach, and all of the key sectors of the community are represented around the table.

Now it is time to plan your strategies and develop your action plans. The most exciting and rewarding moments of your coalition's work will come now, as your ideas are transformed into strategies, programs and activities and put into a comprehensive action plan that will be your guide to implementation.

What is An Action Plan?

An action plan has two steps. First, it provides a framework for the coalition to focus on the issues it wants to address and develop strategies and programs to tackle these issues. Second, action plans record your strategies, programs and activities along with specific action steps for implementation. These include:

- all tasks necessary for implementing the strategy, activity or program;
- specific individuals or groups responsible for each task and;
- clear time frames for the task's completion.

The best action plans are done collaboratively, where representatives of all of the major coalition players are on hand to work together. If everyone can't be in the same room, make sure there are ample opportunities for key actors to review the plan and agree to its contents. An action plan with no agreement can end up being a "non-action" plan!

Why Are Action Plans Important?

Nothing loses steam and involvement faster for a coalition than a lot of talking with no action. Coming up with broad ideas is one thing, but actually developing concrete strategies and getting them implemented is quite another.

When an action plan is in place, both coalition members and the wider community have a mechanism to hold each other accountable to commitments that have been made and to monitor the process of program implementation.

Most importantly, action plans provide a framework to get things done in a timely way and allow for coalition planners to examine the real nuts and bolts of implementation, ensuring greater success for its programs.

Defining Your Planning Issues

Moving from broad goals and objectives to concrete strategies and programs is a difficult but essential step in making your ideas become reality. A problem that many coalitions have is that too much time is spent on the "big picture" of visioning change rather than the specifics of how that change will come about. Before you get down to your specific strategies, however, taking the time to ***break problems down into specific issues*** should come first.

Problems vs. Issues

What Are Problems?

We spend a lot of time in our coalition planning sessions talking about problems: drug abuse, teen pregnancy, lack of citizen power. But despite the overwhelming agreement around the planning table that these problems are the ones we need to tackle, we often have a hard time getting a firm grasp on how we should approach these overwhelming ills.

That's because problems like the ones above and the others your coalition wants to solve often seem too large to address. Talking about problems without breaking them down into "doable" and real pieces creates a feeling of defeat before you even begin. Can your coalition really end drug abuse? Maybe it can, but only if you begin to break the problem of drug abuse down into the "issues" that your coalition really wants to confront.

What Are Issues?

Issues are the particular aspects of the bigger problem that members really want to address. Issues lend themselves to concrete strategies, programs and activities because they are ***specific***. When issues are discussed, they include clear information such as:

- Who (populations)
- What (actions, non-actions)
- Conditions (locations, amounts)
- Why (impact on themselves, others and the community)

Let's take the earlier example of the problem of drug abuse and try to break it down into “issues” for a coalition. Some of the specific “issues” that the coalition may want to address under the larger heading of drug abuse may be:

- High school students who are at “high risk” for dropping out and are using cocaine during after school hours at "Jane Doeville High School"

- Drug selling by an organized group of dealers in vacant lots/ abandoned buildings on Maple and Oak Streets

- Expectant mothers in community “X” using alcohol and tobacco during their pregnancies

Issues vs. Problems

Each of these “issues” clearly lend themselves to different strategies and approaches. The first example may suggest a more school-based approach, the second, law enforcement and youth development and the third, a more education and outreach method. But all of them can fall under the problem of drug abuse. What we’ve done by breaking the problem down is:

- Made the problem less overwhelming and more concrete

- Begun to suggest who needs to be involved in helping to tackle the issue

- Created explicit and measurable "issues" for the coalition to address

By taking this step before you begin action planning, you’ll avoid lengthy, abstract discussions and be ready to get to your real task: creating programs and strategies that will work! Worksheet #2 at the end of this Chapter gives you a tool to take problems and break them down into workable issues.

Creating Strategies And Programs

Now that you have the "issues" around which the coalition will focus its plan, you are ready to begin the process of creating the strategies and programs that will address them. Unlike "visioning" where everyone gets to share their ultimate dreams, a good planning process stays grounded in hard, cold reality.

There are six key questions that need to be examined in order to do effective planning. Each question reveals more and more important information for your planning process and moves you closer to having all of the elements you need to create substantial and competent strategies.

The process outlined below should be done for each issue you are addressing. The best way to accomplish this is to divide your coalition planning group into "teams." Each team takes on an issue and completes the planning process. The more interested in and informed about the issue your "team" members are, the better the planning process will be.

Question #1: What Are the Causes?

Begin by examining the possible *underlying causes* of the issue. Remember to stay grounded and specific in your thinking. Some members may believe that problems like poverty and racism are the real causes of many of the issues you are addressing but don't stop there! Just like with problems, you need to break down these "banner headlines" into specifics.

If we return to the substance abuse example we used earlier, some of the causes for our identified issues might be:

<u>Issue:</u> Drug Selling
Causes:

- Bad security in the buildings and lots where dealing is taking place
- No other viable economic options for young people other than selling drugs in the neighborhood
- Residents on Maple and Oak have historically tolerated street crime and moved away rather than organized to stop it

Issue: Expectant mothers using alcohol and tobacco
Causes:
•Lack of information about the effects of alcohol and tobacco use during pregnancy
•Lack of affordable prenatal care in the community
•Local bars are the only places for people to gather socially in the community

Identifying the possible causes is essential for good planning. No strategy or program is worth its weight if it does not, in some way, end up addressing the causes of the problem it is meant to confront.

Question #2: Who Are the Actors?

An actor is a key community person who can play a role in solving the problem. He or she does not have to be a "formal" leader. Although they may already be in your head, identifying who can be an actor in helping to solve the problem/address the issue is an important step. If your planning "team" is as diverse as it should be and includes representatives from a variety of sectors in your community, someone may have ideas about key actors that are new to you. You want to involve as many essential individuals and institutions as you can to help.

By identifying all of the possible actors, you begin to address an important issue for your planning process beyond just who can help you: community ownership.

Identifying actors addresses the issue of community ownership of your plan. Each actor who is listed may become someone who will eventually need to be invested and "bought in" to your plan in order to make it work. You will want to include ideas for this in your final action plan.

Actors
With our substance abuse issues, some key actors would be:

Drug Selling:
•The young people selling drugs
•Owners of abandoned buildings which are the site of drug sales

•Neighborhood residents who live on Maple and Oak
•Department of Health's Vacant Lot Cleaning Task Force
•Local police captain
•Local businesses and/or banks

Pregnant Mothers Using Alcohol and Tobacco
•The pregnant women
•Mothers/grandmothers of pregnant women
•Bar owners
•Local hospitals and clinics

Don't forget to include the coalition staff, if you have one, as an actor who needs to be invested in the plan in order for it to be a success.

Question #3: What Roles Should the Actors Play?

The individuals and institutions you have listed could play a number of different roles. What we are after here is what they "ideally" could do to help. The key here is to be as creative as you can while still being realistic.

Ideal Roles - Drug Selling

Actor:
Owners of abandoned buildings used as drug sales sites
Ideal roles:
•secure and board up buildings to prevent access
•develop site (turn over to community groups)

Actor:
Neighborhood residents on Maple and Oak
Ideal Roles:
•organize resident/block association to organize for better street lights and law enforcement
•set up information-giving network with local police

Ideal Roles - Pregnant Women Using Alcohol and Tobacco

Actor:
Pregnant women
Ideal roles
•stop using alcohol and tobacco
•get better prenatal care

Actor:
Local hospitals and clinics
Ideal roles:
•make prenatal information and care available and affordable to all women in the community

Identifying "ideal" roles for your actors yields two important points. First, it provides an opportunity to think deeply about what the actor is capable of doing and to be creative about visioning possible new roles and actions. Second, these roles may become key elements of your final strategies.

Remember, don't be exhaustive — every role does not have to be listed. One or two key roles will probably do fine. Too many entries will start to feel overwhelming, so stick to what's important.

Question #4: What Are the Barriers?

Now, we get down to reality. Every good planning process tries to take into account the barriers that may eventually pose themselves and impede implementation.

Focus here on what the barriers are to these actors fulfilling these roles. By anticipating the "walls" that you may have to scale early in the planning process, you ensure two essential things. First, that these "walls" won't rear up during the implementation of your plan and stop its momentum and success. Nothing loses participation and commitment from members faster than having to stop and reevaluate a plan in midstream due to unforeseen obstacles. Second, this step gives you an opportunity to build "barrier breakers" into your strategies or programs. These may include additional resources, training or staff members. Let's visit our "action plan in progress."

ISSUE/PROBLEM:

Drug Dealing

ACTORS people or institutions who can help solve the problem	IDEAL ROLES one or two activities each actor could undertake to help solve the problem	BARRIERS what walls might we run up against/why aren't these activities taking place?
Owners of abandoned buildings	secure buildings to prevent access	absentee owner not interested or can't be found
	develop site (turn over to community group)	owner receiving money from drug dealers developing site too costly
Neighborhood residents	organize resident/ block association	resident fear and apathy
	set up information network with police	

ISSUE/PROBLEM:

Pregnant women who use alcohol and tobacco

ACTORS people or institutions who can help <u>solve</u> the problem	IDEAL ROLES one or two activities each actor could undertake to help solve the problem	BARRIERS what walls might we run up against/why aren't these activities taking place?
Pregnant women	stop using alcohol and tobacco	addiction
	get better prenatal care	lack of education care not available or affordable fear of stigma of being pregnant and going to AA lack of AA and other self help groups
Local hospitals and clinics	make prenatal care and information available and affordable	money constraints (insurance, cost of care delivery) insensitive staff unaware of needs in community

Question #5: What Are the Strategies and Programs?

Now, we are ready to create our strategies and programs. ***Good strategies and programs take into account not only the best way to address the issues but the actors, their roles and barriers.***

ISSUE/PROBLEM:
Drug Dealing

ACTORS people or institutions who can help solve the problem	IDEAL ROLES one or two activities each actor could undertake to help solve the problem	BARRIERS what walls might we run up against/why aren't these activities taking place?	STRATEGIES/PROGRAMS/ACTIVITIES creative, collaborative ways to address problems, overcome barriers
Owners of abandoned buildings	secure buildings to prevent access	absentee owner not interested or can't be found owner receiving money from drug dealers	Research department of buildings to identify owner's name - send letter and petition signed by all neighborhood residents
	develop site (turn over to community group)	developing site too costly	Identify local community organization that could develop the site as a youth center or other community program
Neighborhood residents	organize resident/ block association set up information network with police	resident fear and apathy	target funds for a local organizer to work with residents or work with existing neighborhood organizations

ISSUE/PROBLEM:
Pregnant women who use alcohol and tobacco

ACTORS people or institutions who can help <u>solve</u> the problem	IDEAL ROLES one or two activities each actor could undertake to help solve the problem	BARRIERS what walls might we run up against/why aren't these activities taking place?	STRATEGIES/ PROGRAMS/ ACTIVITIES creative, collaborative ways to address problems, overcome barriers
Pregnant women	stop using alcohol and tobacco	addiction lack of education	Work with local providers to develop AA and other self help groups for pregnant women
Local hospitals and clinics	get better prenatal care make prenatal care and information available and affordable	care not available or affordable and fear of stigma of being pregnant and going to AA lack of AA and other self help groups money constraints (insurance, cost of care delivery) insensitive staff unaware of needs in community	Work with other hospitals and state agencies to identify additional funding sources

This is where you need to bring in all of your members' knowledge, "street smarts" and best creative thinking. Take the time to really look at the specific communities and/or populations you want to focus on and especially what you know works!

Question #6: What Resources Do We Have/Do We Need?

Resources, both human and material, play a key role in planning.

Resources may be staff time, training, physical facilities, community involvement, information or money.

By identifying both the resources you have and those you need, you are really doing two important pieces of work. First, you are identifying some key tasks that must be built in to your action plan, those of obtaining the resources you don't have.

Second, and most important, you are beginning to catalogue one of the key criteria for ***prioritizing*** your strategies and identifying them as *short term* (to be implemented immediately) or *long term* (to be implemented later.) Although resources should not be the only guideline used for making this decision, they are certainly one of the most important.

Checking Back to Causes

You don't want to continue to the next phase of the planning process without this important step. Here, you may find you need to do some adjusting and rethinking of your strategies as you check them against the underlying causes of the issues that you identified earlier.

The important question here is "Do the strategies and programs you have designed address the causes?" It is improbable that the answer will be 100% yes. The important point now is that the members of your "team" are satisfied with the results so far.

Concluding This Phase of Planning

Now is the time for "checking back" with each other! If you have been working in separate "teams," you should come together and report on and compare the work you have done. Look for duplications of strategies and programs and make sure all of the members of the coalition agree before moving on!

It may take some time to review all of the work that has been done. That's fine. It is through this process that true "buy-in" takes place. If anyone is feeling that their input and/or issues have not been considered or is opposed to a program that has been suggested, now is the time to know and negotiate. Worksheet #3 outlines this process for you to use with your coalition.

Action Planning With Your Coalition

The planning process is now only half finished. It is time to take your program ideas and put them into an action plan for implementation. This may require splitting up into "teams" again or it may be done by the coalition planners as a whole.

Your final action plan will have each strategy/program listed, the **tasks** necessary to implement these strategies, **assigned responsibility** for each task to an individual or organization and an **established time frame** for each task to be accomplished.

Identifying Tasks

Now each strategy, program, or activity must be broken down into concrete tasks that need to be carried out in order to ensure the most effective implementation. Tasks are usually divided into three categories:

- *Outreach*

Outreach tasks may include: reaching out to key actors who have been identified during the planning process but have not been involved with the coalition to date; organizing public meetings or events and media/press outreach.

- *Resource Gathering*

Resource gathering tasks may include: researching funding sources; looking for physical facilities; hiring additional staff or finding the people needed for a door-to-door survey.

- *Program*

Program tasks include: training, program implementation steps, evaluation and staff development.

Each task should be listed on your action plan under the heading of a strategy or program.

Assigning Responsibility

Each task should have an individual or organization designated to carry it out. All of the concrete tasks in the world won't get carried out unless someone is responsible to see that they do.

It is important that you do not assign a task unless the responsibility has been accepted. This can create a host of negative feelings and significant disinvestment. If you are sure that "it won't be a problem, I'll just tell her at the next meeting," you may want to check first anyway. You can save yourself a lot of heartache.

Establishing Time Frames

Each task must now be assigned a time frame or "due date" for its completion. This step should never be left out. Worksheet #4 provides an action plan outline.

The most important thing to remember is to be realistic. If you are anxious to initiate a program, it won't really start any sooner if you set unrealistic early dates for the program to be activated and the tasks accomplished. What you will probably have is disappointed people who were given unrealistic expectations. Avoid this if you can.

Allow the time necessary for each task to be done well. It will make the program stronger and create more faith in the coalition that planning is done on a realistic and genuine level.

Key Points

- Action plans have two steps. The first is to provide a framework for the coalition to focus on the issues it wants to address and the second is to provide a guide for implementation.

- It is essential to break down "problems" into concrete and specific "issues." Issues are the pieces of the bigger problem that lend themselves to concrete strategies, programs and activities because they are **specific** and include clear information necessary for effective planning such as: Who (populations), What (actions and non-actions), Conditions (locations, amounts) and Why (impact on themselves, others and the community.)

- When developing strategies and programs, six key questions must be answered: What are the causes of the issue/ problem? Who are the actors? What roles should they play? What are the barriers? What are the programs and strategies? What resources do we have/do we need?

- The final phase of the action plan includes: specific tasks, assigned responsibility for each task and established time frames for completing them. There are three categories of tasks: Outreach, Resource gathering and Program. This last step creates an accountablity system within the coalition and between the coalition and the community and a framework to get things done in a timely, efficient and effective way.

Worksheet #1

Sample Agenda for an Action Planning Meeting

Instructions:

*The best results for action planning will probably come from a **facilitated** meeting where one person, the facilitator, guides the whole group through the steps of action planning. This agenda should be used as a guide for an action planning meeting.*

Build breaks of 10-20 minutes into the meeting agenda.

Establish clear time frames for the whole meeting and for each item on the agenda.

Don't limit discussion too much. People need to feel that their ideas and insights have been included and heard.

Action Planning Meeting Agenda

1. Welcome and Introductions
2. Overview of the Action Planning Framework
3. Identifying "Problems" and "Issues"
4. Action Planning Teams: Developing Strategies and Programs
5. Team Reports: What Have We Developed?/Adjustments
6. Establishing the Final Action Plan: Tasks, Assignments and Time Frames
7. Getting Agreement on the Plan

Worksheet #2

Problems and Issues

Problem: ____

____

____

Who *(population where the problem exists/that you want to target)* BE AS SPECIFIC AS POSSIBLE:

____

____

____

Conditions *(locations where the activities are occurring, amounts, etc.)*:

____

____

____

Whys *(impact of activities on the target population, on others and the community)*

____

____

PROBLEM SOLVING WORKSHEET

ISSUE/PROBLEM:

ACTORS people or institu-tions who can help <u>solve</u> the problem	IDEAL ROLES one or two activities each actor could undertake to help solve the problem	BARRIERS what "walls" might we run up against/why aren't these activities taking place?	STRATEGIES/PROGRAMS/ ACTIVITIES creative, collaborative ways to address problems, overcome barriers	RESOURCES needed to effectively implement strategies H = have N = need

Worksheet #4

Action Plan

STRATEGY:

ACTIONS TO BE TAKEN (TASKS)	BY WHOM	BY WHEN	I/WE NEED...

CHAPTER 10

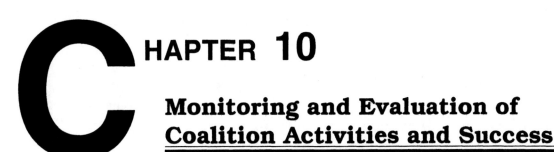

Monitoring and Evaluation of Coalition Activities and Success

by Stephen Fawcett, Ph.D., David Foster, Ph.D, and Vincent Francisco

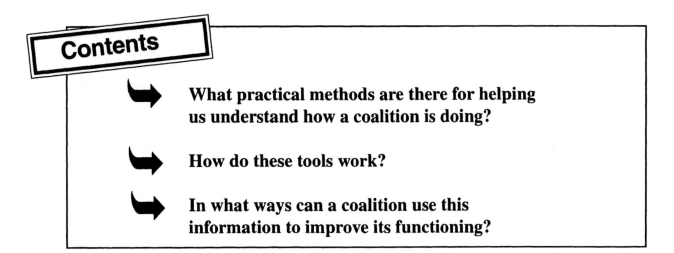

Contents

- What practical methods are there for helping us understand how a coalition is doing?
- How do these tools work?
- In what ways can a coalition use this information to improve its functioning?

Background

Coalitions are alliances among different organizations or community members to achieve a common purpose. They represent an increasingly common strategy for encouraging collaborative problem solving with a variety of issues of community interest. Until recently, coalitions used relatively few financial resources to coordinate the efforts of professionals and community members. Little time or energy was spent in evaluating coalition process or outcome, and few practical methods were available to assess whether coalitions were functioning effectively.

More recently, private foundations, such as the W. K. Kellogg Foundation and the Robert Wood Johnson Foundation, and government agencies, such as the U.S. Center for Substance Abuse Prevention, have invested greater financial resources into coalition development. As concerns with accountability have grown, there have been some efforts to develop appropriate methods for monitoring and evaluating community coalitions — to understand their development and improve their function. Perhaps more importantly, a coalition evaluation must be useful to the coalition staff and membership.

Why Evaluate Your Coalition?

Why evaluate your coalition?

Because you, coalition members, and community members may have a number of questions about your coalition that you cannot readily answer. These questions might include:

- Is the coalition doing anything?
- Is the coalition making a difference?
- How much has the coalition accomplished in the past year?
- Is this coalition focused on internal issues (e.g. how members get along with each other) or on external issues (e.g. changing policies and practices of community agencies relative to its mission)?
- Which committees or coalition members are most active?
- What did the coalition do to accomplish X, Y and Z objectives?

There may be other questions in which funding agents may be especially interested, such as: “Can the value of the evaluation be increased by giving information back to coalitions for use in improving their functioning?" and "What key features of successful coalitions are the most important," and "Can they be copied to produce other successful coalitions?”

University of Kansas Work Group Model

In 1990, researchers at the Work Group on Health Promotion and Community Development at the University of Kansas developed a monitoring and evaluation system for community coalitions (Fawcett, Paine, Francisco, & Vliet, 1993; Francisco, Paine, & Fawcett, 1993). Based on earlier work, this system was developed and field-tested in several different contexts: with Project Freedom, a substance abuse coalition in a city of 300,000 funded by the Kansas Health Foundation; with the Decade of Hope, a coalition of the Jicarilla Apache Tribe funded by the U.S. Center for Substance Abuse Prevention; and with Kansas LEAN, a coalition for the prevention of cardiovascular disease funded by the Kansas Health Foundation. In 1991, the Work Group and AHEC Community Partners began collaborating to adapt this system for use with eight health and human service coalitions across Massachusetts supported by funds from the Kellogg Foundation. Since that time, the system has been adopted by evaluators working with a number of other community coalitions. The system described below was designed to understand the functioning of a coalition, and provide a means to enhance the coalition's functioning in ways that the coalition membership and funding agents would value. As these methods have been adapted in a variety of situations, the ideal of enhancing the capacity of a community is served.

There are several aspects of this monitoring and evaluation system that can be of general use to coalitions, detailed in a recently published manual (Fawcett and Associates, 1993). The system involves several key measurement instruments, including: a) the monitoring system, b) critical events analysis (interviews with key informants), and c) surveys of coalition members and interested parties. Each section includes a discussion of how information is collected and how it can be used to address key evaluation questions.

Monitoring System

The monitoring system is the primary means by which information about coalition process and outcome is collected and reported. It is a system of tracking what a coalition does by examination of meeting minutes, interviews with key coalition members, and monthly activity logs completed by some coalition members. Several important features are described: key measures, event logs, and graphing and feedback, along with illustrative data and ideas for using the monitoring data.

Table 1

Planning Products (PP) are accomplishments within the coalition that contribute to its effectiveness as an organization, such as: completion of a mission statement, adoption of by-laws, establishment of a task force, completion of an annual report or member survey.

Community Actions (CA) are coalition actions which engage directly with the "target" of a desired change that is part of a coalition goal. This "target" may be an individual or an organization, and may or may not be a part of the coalition. Examples might include: meeting with the newspaper editor to discuss improving media coverage of health or human service concerns, meeting with the police chief to support adoption of community policing, or the Multi-Cultural Committee writing to an agency director advocating that the agency hire bilingual staff.

Community Changes (CC) are those changes in programs, policies or practices in the community that are, at least in part, the result of the coalition pursuing one or more of its goals. These include: changes in the services and resources available to the community; changes in the rules by which things are done, and/or the way they are done. Examples would be: a change in hospital policy regarding the provision of interpreters for patients who are not comfortable communicating in English; the creation of a community's first information and referral guide to assist people in finding services; the establishment of a new community development organization in a neighborhood.

Services Provided (SP) are activities completed by the coalition that provide an educational, or other type of, service to individuals or groups outside the coalition, such as: the distribution of a resource directory in the community, an educational program on immigration rules, a community forum on affordable housing, etc.

Resources Generated (RG) are resources secured for use by the coalition to support its own development, to provide services, or for the use of others in the community. These resources may be financial resources or services or materials donated by individuals or groups for which they would normally be paid or reimbursed. Examples include: a grant to pay the salary of a part-time coalition staff person, a lawyer donated time to present a workshop on immigration laws, an agency donates a staff person's time to prepare and distribute the newsletter.

Key measures.

The monitoring system is used to capture five key aspects of coalition process and outcome: a) planning products, b) community actions, c) community changes, d) services provided, and e) financial resources generated. Table 1 provides operational definitions and examples for each type of event.

Note that each recorded event is at least potentially important to the coalition. Planning products — such as a detailed action plan — may be the end result of many weeks of planning activities. Community actions — such as lobbying a key elected official — provide the most sensitive indicator of community interaction and mobilization. Community changes — a new program, policy, or practice related to the mission — provide a strong indicator of community empowerment. Services provided — such as publications or workshops — may help the coalition to become better known and/or attract new members. Finally, financial resources generated — such as grants received — provide evidence of the financial sustainability of the coalition.

Event logs. Event logs are used to record the five key aspects of coalition process and outcome described in Table 1. A sample event log is shown in Worksheet #1. Each coalition event that fits into any of these five categories is described with information about: a) who did what?, b) what happened as a result?, c) why was the event important?, d) what organizations were collaborators? e) what objective did this relate to?, and f) was this the first time such an event had happened? Event logs are completed by well-informed members of the coalition, such as coalition staff and leadership of active committees or task forces. If the coalition has an "outside" evaluator, the logs are completed and forwarded to the evaluator monthly; otherwise they are processed by a trained coalition member who agrees to compile and report the results. Conversations with those who filled out the forms are used to clarify information provided and to check for completeness. Worksheets #2 and #3 show other ways of gathering this data.

Graphing and feedback. Each instance of the above events is recorded on a graph as one unit, such as getting the newspaper to assign a reporter to cover human services, or having the board of the local housing authority adopt a pilot program in tenant self-management. A member of the "evaluation team" who has been trained in applying the definitions (Francisco, Paine, & Fawcett, 1993) then gives the proper code (PP, CA, CC, SP or RG) to each reported event. Graphs of each type of event are drawn cumulatively; that is, the graph increases over time to show the addition of each new event. Cumulative graphs highlight trends: the more steeply the line goes up, the more activity; a flat line shows no new occurrences of the event in that series of months.

These data and graphs have been given to the coalition to analyze. In the first year of the coalition, data is given to the coalition monthly, and quarterly thereafter. We have found it to be more appropriate to give more feedback early in the life of the coalition, and that less is needed once the coalition is established. When this information is given to coalition leadership, board members, and funding partners, it provides an opportunity to review coalition progress and accomplishment. Accomplishments, such as a new policy change or grant obtained, are celebrated. Patterns of little or no growth (as judged by the reduction in slope of the line on the graph) are also discussed, with attention to how the coalition can become more successful in meeting its aims (an increase in the slope of the line). Since each coalition operates with different aims and context, coalitions should not be compared on their levels of accomplishment. Rather, graphing and feedback enables the leadership and staff of each coalition to see how they are doing relative to their own expectations and those of their membership and funding partners.

Illustrative data. Figures 1 and 2 show the data that came from using this monitoring and evaluation system with two community coalitions. The data illustrate different developmental patterns that can be expected.

Figure 1 is a graph of a well-functioning coalition, showing a composite of all five features. Notice the relatively consistent growth in all measures over time. Also note what may be a characteristic developmental sequence for effective coalitions: coalition planning develops ahead of community actions, which, in turn, precede community changes. For this particular coalition, providing services and generating financial resources have been rather secondary.

Figure 2 displays a somewhat more ambiguous situation. Although planning is occurring at a high and steady rate, there is little movement with community actions and other important measures of coalition functioning (as evidenced by a several month long flat spot on the line). It is important that coalition leaders and staff, with the support of consultants when available, consider this data carefully and decide what support may be needed to help the group bring about desired community change associated with its mission.

Figure 1

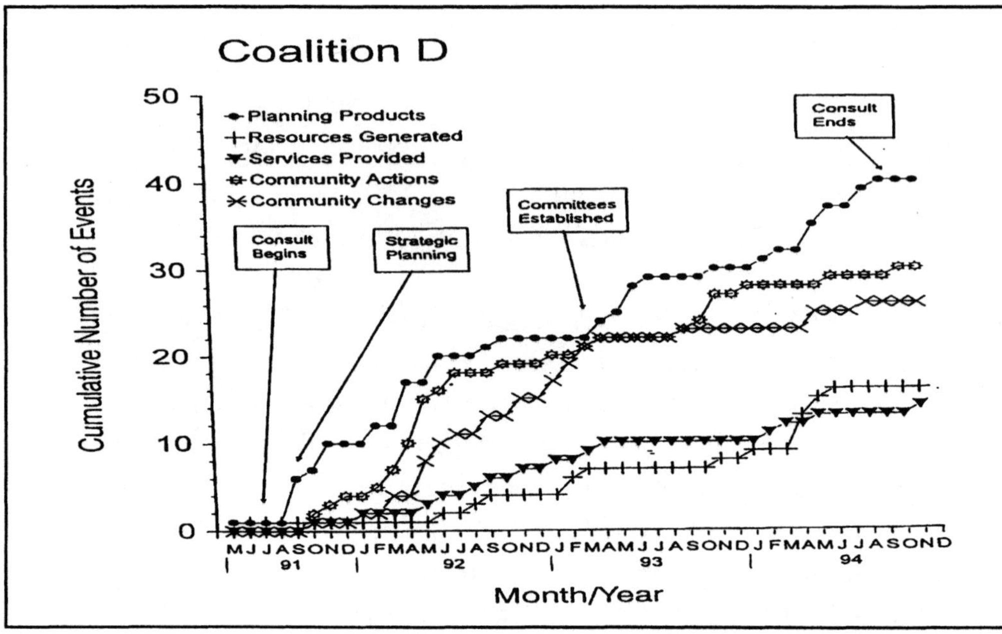

Figure 2

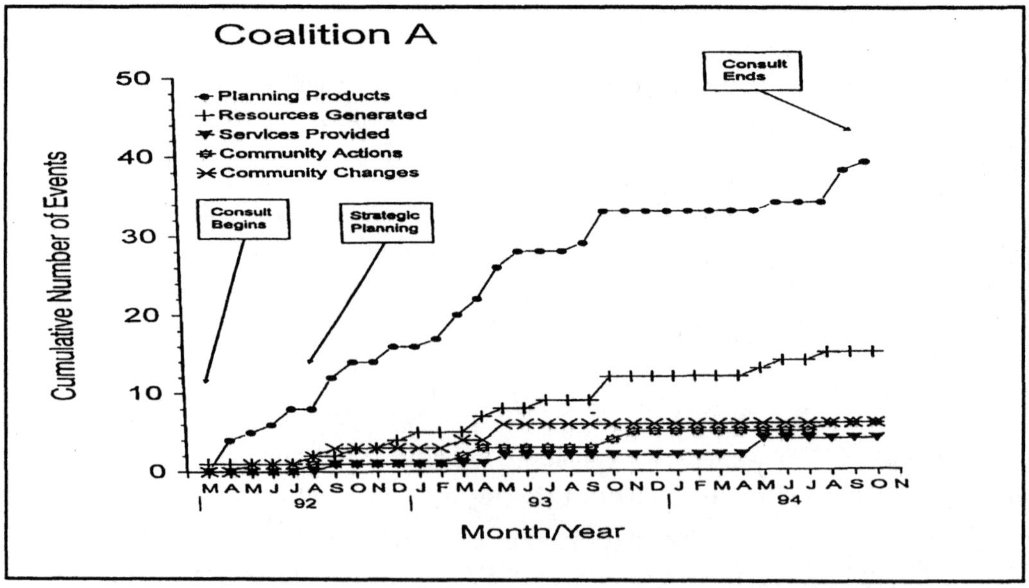

Using the monitoring data. The data yielded from the monitoring system help address several key questions. For example, "Is the coalition doing anything?," consider presenting information about the amount and rate of planning products and community actions. To the question "Is the coalition making a difference?," consider presenting data on community changes and services provided.

Analysis of Critical Events. An analysis of critical events in the life of the coalition (using interviews with key participants, such as the 3-4 most active leaders and staff) can provide an understanding and record of important events in the coalition's history. This section outlines the process used to identify and examine key events, integration of these data with the quantitative information from the monitoring system, and uses of the information about critical events.

Interview process. Structured interview questions, such as "What are the most important things that have happened in the history of the coalition?," are used to identify critical events, and their timing, from the perspective of key participants. Additional questions are also used to examine each identified key event: a) the reason for its importance, b) the situation or conditions in which it occurred, c) key actions and actors, d) barriers and resistance, e) key resources, f) consequences for the coalition, and g) consequences for the community as a whole. The interviews conclude with a discussion of overall lessons and future directions for the coalition. Worksheet #2 provides the outline used to conduct these structured interviews with key participants.

These data are compiled and consolidated into a narrative report and events timeline. A draft of this report is reviewed by the key participants for factual and presentation errors before a final report is submitted to the coalition for its use.

Using the information about critical events. The data yielded from the interviews also helps address key questions. What factors seem to contribute positively to coalition functioning? Look at the associations between identified critical events, such as completed action plans, and corresponding increases in key measures, such as community actions and community changes. What factors seem to contribute negatively to coalition functioning? Consider the associations between factors, such as loss of key staff and a corresponding inactivity in key measures.

Integrating quantitative and qualitative data. This qualitative information from the interviews helps give meaning to the quantitative information gathered through the monitoring system. By overlaying each critical event on graphs of key measures we can see which ones seem related to noticeable increases in the measures (steeper slopes), or to reduced activity (flatter lines). These can then be included in the graphs to show how they fit together. For example, as Figure 3 shows, we often see an increase in the rate of community actions (and eventually community changes) following strategic planning events. Although a cause and effect relationship is not proven, when these and other associations are found repeatedly, they help suggest important factors that contribute to effective coalition functioning.

Combinations of these data can be reported in a variety of formats. Within the coalition, they offer the grounds for celebrating accomplishments and for reassessing shortfalls. They can also be useful in establishing the coalition's credibility with other groups, including public officials and funders. Worksheets #4 and #5 show two styles for reporting data.

Figure 3

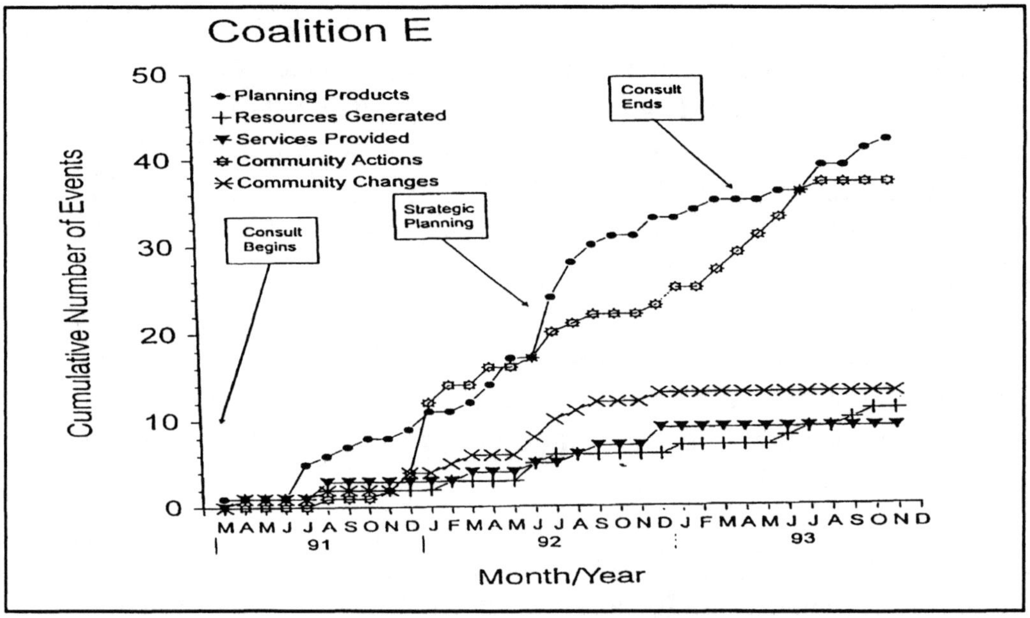

Constituent Surveys. There are two surveys that can be administered periodically to all the coalition's key constituents, such as the full membership and funding partners. The first survey — an Annual Membership Satisfaction Survey — includes questions about satisfaction with the coalition's planning, leadership, services, community involvement, and progress toward accomplishing goals. Specific items ask about satisfaction with such aspects as the strength and competence of staff, training and technical assistance, and diversity of coalition membership. The survey provides members with an opportunity to share their views about how the coalition is doing, through both the rating of items and sections for open-ended comments. (See the example in Worksheet #6.)

The second survey — a Constituency Survey of Outcomes — asks coalition members, funders and outside experts to rate the significance of changes the project has made in the community (Community Changes, as reflected in the monitoring logs). This allows a somewhat independent rating of how important one change in the community is relative to other community changes accomplished by the coalition. The survey also asks respondents to rate the overall importance of these changes in achieving the coalition's mission. (See the example in Worksheet #7.) This will allow the coalition to reflect on what they did, and provide them with an opportunity to assess future changes proposed by the coalition and perhaps make changes in the proposed objectives to emphasize those changes which may make a greater contribution to accomplishment of the coalition's mission.

Survey process. The survey instrument for "Member Satisfaction" is generic and can be used as is, or with some modifications if desired, by a variety of coalitions. The "Survey of Outcomes" provides a format that must be adapted by each coalition to include its particular community changes and dates of accomplishment

These surveys can be distributed by mail to all members of the coalition and to important funding partners, preferably with a self-addressed, stamped envelope enclosed. An alternative strategy that can increase the response rate and reduce costs is to take time at a coalition meeting to have attenders fill out the survey, and then to mail copies to those who are absent and those outside the coalition.

Satisfaction data are summarized to give the average ratings and range of responses for each survey item, and a summary of the written comments. Outcome data are summarized by rank ordering the results, showing those community changes seen as the most significant through the least.

Using the survey data. By focusing on items rated as especially high or low, coalition leadership can examine and better act upon the coalition's strengths and problems. This is especially true if there are patterns to the high and low scores. For the Satisfaction data, examples include: quality of leadership items are rated consistently low, or items related to coalition communication are rated quite high. For the Outcome data: symbolic actions (such as a rally in front of city hall) may be rated as less significant than the creation of new policies or programs. For coalition leaders, often the most helpful feedback from the Satisfaction survey lies in the written comments, if members are able to express their feelings freely.

Overall Summary

This chapter outlined a practical system for monitoring and evaluating community coalitions. Its methods and uses are presented, along with illustrations from actual community coalitions.

This methodology is particularly helpful in assessing the process and intermediate outcomes of community coalitions. To assess ultimate impacts, behavioral and community — level indicators specific to the particular mission — such as prevention of substance abuse — should also be used. For the example of substance abuse prevention, behavioral indicators may be the amount of self reported substance abuse as determined by a survey of high school seniors, and community level indicators might include the number of alcohol-related single vehicle nighttime crashes in the community.

The ultimate standard for coalition evaluation is its ability to be used. This system has been designed to contribute to better understanding of how coalitions function. By emphasizing the importance of feeding data back to coalitions, the methods can also contribute directly to the coalitions' functioning. As these methods are adapted for use in a variety of contexts, the ideal of enhancing the capacity of a community is served.

Event Log

Advocacy Organization

Site:__________________ Recorder:______________________ Reporting Period - From__________To:________

Using this form, please describe: 1) actions taken to bring about changes in the community that are related to reducing substance abuse, and 2) changes in *programs* (e.g., peer-led support groups), *policies* (e.g. new ordinance increasing fines for selling tobacco to minors), and *practices* (e.g. increased enforcement of laws against selling alcohol to minors) that are related to reducing substance abuse.

Date (Month/ Year)	Event	Description
	a. New (or change in) strategic plan, committee, etc. b. New (or change in) program or service c. Action to bring about new program or service d. New (or change in) policy e. Action to bring about new policy f. New (or change in) practice g. Action to bring about new practice	a. Who did what? b. What happened as a result? c. Why was it important? d. What organizations were collaborators? e. What community sector or objective does this relate to? f. Was this the first time this event happened?

Send this form by the first Friday of every month to: Work Group, Attn: Project Freedom Replication Initiative, 4086 Dole Center, University of Kansas, Lawrence, KS 66045

Format for Key Participant Interviews

Organization: ______________________________

Participant: ______________________________

Participant's Position: ______________________________

Participant's Involvement with the Organization: ______________________________

____

Date of Interview: ______________________________

Interviewer: ______________________________

Interview Process:

Ask introductory questions.... What key events or incidents were critical to the Organization's development? Its major accomplishments or successes? Its setbacks or challenges?

After listening to the participant and taking notes on this page, identify the several particularly important events. State these to the participant, asking for agreement about them. Each identified critical event will be considered using the form that follows.

Critical Events:

Worksheet

Critical Event

Date of the Event:

Rationale... *Why was this event particularly important?*

Context or Conditions... *What was going on at the time of the event? What made the conditions right for this to happen?*

Key Actions and Actors... *What key actions brought about the critical event? Who were the key actors?*

Barriers and Resistance... *Were the group's actions met with barriers or resistance? What types of barriers? Who resisted?*

Key Resources... *What key resources (people, financial resources, political influence, etc.) were used to bring about the critical event? How were these resources used to overcome barriers and resistance?*

Consequences (Organization)... *What were the consequences of or results of the critical event for the Organization?*

Consequences (Community)... *What were the consequences for the community?*

Overall Lessons... *Overall, what lessons have you learned from your involvement with the Organization? What lessons have you learned from the Organization's attempts to define and act on its mission?*

Future Directions... *What issues does the Organization face in the future? What challenges should be addressed?*

Worksheet

Advocacy Organization

Site:______________ Recorder:______________ Reporting Period - From:__________ To:__________

Media Coverage (Please attach copies of any articles)			
Date (Month/Year)	Topic of Media Coverage (News report, Feature story)	Media Type (Newspaper, TV, Radio, etc.)	Number of Newspaper Column Inches or Broadcast Minutes

Dollars Obtained		
Date (Month/Year)	Source	Dollar Amount

Resources Generated For example: Grants, contacts, and in-kind donations (e.g. free professional service)		
Date (Month/Year)	Source	Dollar Amount or Equivalent

Send this form by the first Friday of every month to: Work Group, Attn: Project Freedom Replication Initiative, 4086 Dole Center, University of Kansas, Lawrence, KS 66045

Ongoing Services Provided

Advocacy Organization

Site:____________________ Recorder:____________ Reporting Period - From:________ To:________

Using this form, please describe classes, workshops, newsletter, screenings, or other informational or service programs provided to community members. Please note whether this is the first time that this service has been provided in the community.

Date (Month/Year)	Ongoing Service (e.g., workshop, class, screening)	Location of Service	Number of people attending	New Service? Yes/No

Send this form by the first Friday of every month to: Work Group, Attn: Project Freedom Replication Initiative, 4086 Dole Center, University of Kansas, Lawrence, KS 66045

Worksheet #4

ANYTOWN COMMUNITY COALITION

Coalition Accomplishments

- **Created new Anytown Community Coalition**
  - Built Coalition organization
    - Established committees
    - Elected officers
    - Adopted mission statement and goals
    - Produced informational brochure about the Coalition
  - Received financial support from Town Meeting
- **Generated new resources**
  - Grant/services from Community Partners/Kellogg Foundation
  - Fund raising and grant for Seniors Day
- **Sponsored new services and opportunities**
  - Presented Legislative Forum on elder issues
  - Organized first annual Seniors Day attended by 125 seniors
- **Promoted changes in community programs and systems**
  - Transit survey led to Anytown Bus service changes
  - Stimulated creation of the Teen Meeting Room
  - Developed/strengthened networking system among providers
  - Reduced duplication of effort in responding to community issues
  - Created new opportunities for collaborative projects

Important Work in Progress

- Developing a volunteer clearinghouse
- Creating a unified Community Resource Directory
- Producing a Community Activities Calendar
- Publishing a community transporation "Ride Guide"

Worksheet #5

REPORTING DATA

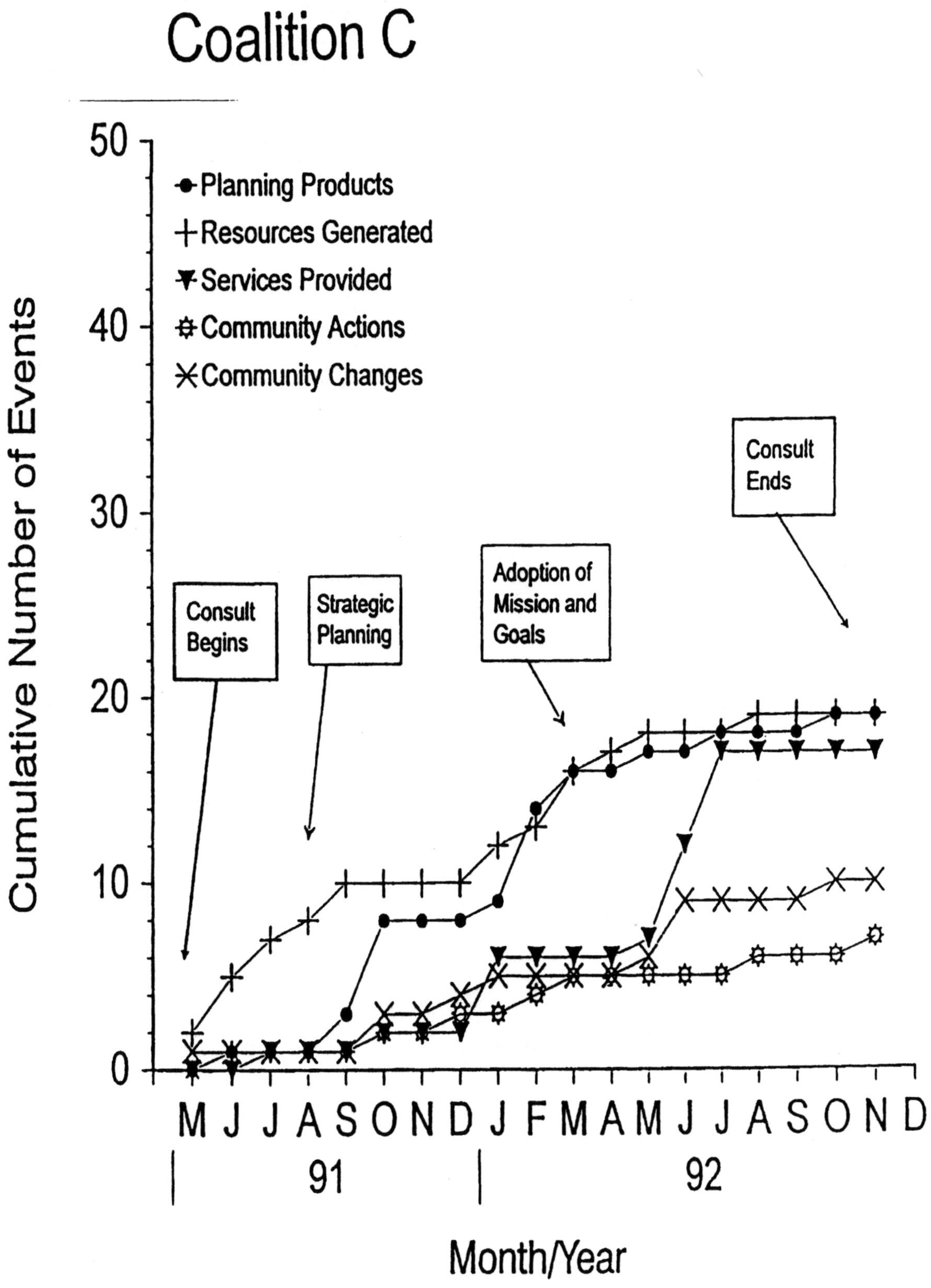

ANNUAL SATISFACTION SURVEY FOR COMMUNITY PARTNERS COALITIONS

We welcome your feedback on how well this coalition is doing. For each item, please circle the number that best shows your satisfaction with that aspect of the coalition. Provide additional comments if you wish.

Your SATISFACTION with the...

PLANNING AND IMPLEMENTATION:

	very dissatisfied				very satisfied
1. Clarity of the vision for where the Coalition should be going	1	2	3	4	5
2. Planning process used to prepare the Coalition's objectives	1	2	3	4	5
3. Follow through on Coalition activities	1	2	3	4	5
4. Strength and competence of staff	1	2	3	4	5
5. Efforts to promote collaborative action	1	2	3	4	5
6. Processes used to assess the community's needs	1	2	3	4	5
7. Training and technical assistance provided by AHEC staff	1	2	3	4	5

Comments:

Worksheet

Your SATISFACTION with the...

LEADERSHIP:

	very dissatisfied				very satisfied
8. Strength and competence of Coalition leadership	1	2	3	4	5
9. Sensitivity to cultural issues	1	2	3	4	5
10. Opportunities for Coalition members to take leadership roles	1	2	3	4	5
11. Willingness of members to take leadership roles	1	2	3	4	5
12. Trust that Coalition members afford each other	1	2	3	4	5

Comments:

Your SATISFACTION with the..

COMMUNITY INVOLVEMENT IN THE COALITION:

	very dissatisfied				very satisfied
13. Participation of influential people from key sectors of the community	1	2	3	4	5
14. Participation of community residents	1	2	3	4	5
15. Diversity of coalition membership	1	2	3	4	5
16. Help given the community in meeting its needs	1	2	3	4	5

17. Help given community groups to become better able to address and resolve their concerns	1	2	3	4	5
18. Efforts in getting funding for community programs	1	2	3	4	5

Comments:

Your SATISFACTION with the...

COMMUNICATION	very dissatisfied				very satisfied
19. Use of the media to promote awareness of the Coalition's goals, actions, and accomplishments	1	2	3	4	5
20. Communication among members of the Coalition	1	2	3	4	5
21. Communication between the Coalition and the broader community	1	2	3	4	5
22. Extent to which Coalition members are listened to and heard	1	2	3	4	5
23. Working relationships established with elected officials	1	2	3	4	5
24. Information provided on issues and available resources	1	2	3	4	5

Comments:

Worksheet

Your SATISFACTION with the...

PROGRESS AND OUTCOME:	very dissatisfied				very satisfied
25. Progress in meeting the Coalition's objectives	1	2	3	4	5
26. Success in generating resources for the Coalition	1	2	3	4	5
27. Fairness with which funds and opportunities are distributed	1	2	3	4	5
28. Capacity of members to give support to each other	1	2	3	4	5
29. Capacity of the Coalition and its members to advocate effectively	1	2	3	4	5
30. Coalition's contribution to improving health and human services in the community	1	2	3	4	5

Comments:

Worksheet

January 27, 1997

Dear Coalition Member:

The purpose of the attached consumer satisfaction questionnaire is to get your feedback on how well this coalition is doing. As you know, this coalition's mission is to ...

Please complete each question by circling the number that best shows your satisfaction with that aspect of the coalition. We welcome additional comments and suggestions you have for improving this coalition..

To protect anonymity, please use the enclosed envelope to return your completed questionnaire to our coalition's evaluators, the Work Group on Health Promotion and Community Development.

Thanks in advance for your valuable advice and feedback.

Best regards,

OVERALL APPROVAL RATING:

Is the community better off today because of this Coalition? (please check one)

Yes _____

No ______

Overall Comments and Suggestions for Improvement:

Thanks for your valuable feedback. Please use the attached envelope to return the completed questionnaire to: Community Partners, 24 South Prospect Street, Amherst, MA 01002

Sample Format for an
Advocacy Outcome Survey
for a Youth Violence Initiative

Advocacy Organization staff and members have been involved in efforts that resulted in a variety of community changes related to youth violence. This survey lists four community changes that resulted from the organization's efforts. For each survey item, please circle the number that best describes how important each community change is to the organization's mission of reducing youth violence. Use the following scale to rate your answers.

1	2	3	4	5
Very Unimportant	Unimportant	Neither Unimportant nor Important	Important	Very Important

Community Changes	IMPORTANCE of the community change to the mission of reducing youth violence				
1. Establish graffiti removal program (8/93)	1	2	3	4	5
2. Change policy regarding punishment for drive-by shootings (9/93)	1	2	3	4	5
3. Establish after-school program for 20 at-risk youth (11/93)	1	2	3	4	5
4. Establish school-business mentoring project for 100 high school students (12/93).	1	2	3	4	5

CHAPTER 11

Resources

Coalition Building Resource Materials

It seems that every time a new coalition gets started, we begin the process of reinventing the wheel. It has been devilishly difficult for those in communities across the country to put their fingers on well-written, useful materials that can help them and their coalition members. In working with numerous coalitions across the country, we have been able to narrow the materials we recommend to a few brief, affordable, and readable handbooks that can be extremely helpful for coalitions.

1) *Community Development, Community Participation and Substance Abuse Prevention by David Chavis and Paul Florin*

This twenty-five page pamphlet, developed for the Prevention Office of Drug Abuse Services in San Jose, California, helps lay out the theoretical understanding behind community development and community participation as they relate to substance abuse prevention. Chavis and Florin define the key concepts regarding community development, and then indicate the key reasons why the community development approach to substance abuse can be especially helpful. Basing their writings on the latest research and literature, these two short papers provide a key rationale and set of definitions for those developing substance abuse prevention coalitions. This is a must read for Substance Abuse Coalitions. Community Development, Community Participation and Substance Abuse Prevention ($5.00 p.pd.) is available from the Bureau of Drug Abuse Services, 645 South Bascom Ave., Building H-10, San Jose, CA, 95128. Published in May of 1990.

2) *The Community Collaboration Manual by The National Assembly of National Voluntary Health and Social Welfare Organizations*

This 76-page manual is extremely well written and very clear with many helpful tables and figures. It leads the reader through the process of collaboration, defining collaboration, talking about start-up, building the collaboration, maintaining the momentum, youth involvement, business involvement, and the role of the media. An example of this manual's helpful tips include their seven keys to successful collaboration: shared vision, skilled leadership, process orientation, cultural diversity, membership-driven agenda, multiple sectors, and accountability. Although somewhat more expensive ($12.95), it is packed with good ideas and good models. It is extremely helpful. To order a copy, make a check payable to "The National Assembly", and write to Collaboration Manual, The National Assembly, 1319 F Street NW, Suite 601, Washington, DC 20004. Published in 1991.

3) *Coalition Building: One Path to Empowered Communities by Thomas Wolff*

This 37-page paper, written by Tom Wolff, is based on eight years of coalition-building experience in Massachusetts. It highlights characteristics of dysfunctional helping systems (fragmentation, duplication of effort, competition, multi-cultural insensitivity, etc.), characteristics of competent helping systems (coordination, cooperation, cultural relevance, etc.) and the coalition-building strategies needed to move towards greater competence. The paper lays the groundwork for the purpose and direction of coalition building. The author defines healthy and competent communities as the ultimate goals of coalition building and community development activities. Case studies, drawn from the author's direct experiences, give examples of how coalitions can succeed. Available for $10.00 from Community Partners, 24 South Prospect Street, Amherst, MA 01002. Published 1991.

4) *Communities Working Collaboratively For A Change by Arthur Turovh Himmelman (July, 1992 Edition)*

Himmelman does an outstanding job of defining collaboration and distinguishing it from networking, coordination and cooperation. He describes two kinds of multi-sectoral collaboration - collaborative betterment and collaborative empowerment and articulates both in a very helpful model. He then goes on to lay out his own model for collaborative empowerment. Excellent, thought-provoking paper from a citizen-participation-government perspective. Cost for this monograph is $10.00 p.pd. To order, please contact: The Himmelman

Consulting Group, 1406 West Lake Street, Suite 209, Minneapolis, MN 55408.

5) *Resources From The Work Group On Health Promotion and Community Development by Steve Fawcett, Adrienne Paine-Andrews, Vince Francisco*

The Work Group on Health Promotion and Community Development is producing some of the best materials for coalition building in the country, including:

Preventing Substance Abuse: An Action Planning Guide for Community-Based Initiatives and **Preventing Adolescent Pregnancy**: An Action Planning Guide for Community-Based Initiatives. These are excellent step-by-step guides that take a coalition through the planning stages including identifying community changes in each sector of the community. Superb manuals, $12 each, p.pd.

Evaluation Handbook: Evaluating and Supporting Initiatives for Community Health and Development. This manual begins with an overview of The Work Group's system for successfully evaluating community health initiatives, including coalitions. Each measurement instrument, its form and instructions, are explained and sampled, and sample data is given in a presentation form (graphs or summary reports). Blank forms are included. $25, p.pd.

Write to: The Work Group, University of Kansas, 4001 Dole Building, Lawrence, KS 66045.

6) *What Makes It Work: A Review of Research Literature On Factors Influencing Successful Collaboration, August, 1992, 53 pages.*

This is a very thorough literature review on coalition building and collaboration done by the Wilder Research Center in St. Paul, Minnesota. It is the only complete literature review we have seen, and at least updates what has been written about coalitions until August of 1992. Rather than reinvent the wheel, start with this publication, and catch up on recent publications since much has been published in the last two years. $11.95

Write to: Wilder Research Center, 1295 Bandana Blvd, #210, St. Paul, MN 55108-5197.

7) *Building Communities From The Inside Out : A path toward finding and mobilizing a community's assets by John Kretzman and John McKnight.*

John McKnight's writing has been an inspiration to coalition builders and community developers for many years. This newest addition to the McKnight library is outstanding. Up to this point, McKnight has been an insightful critic of what is wrong with the health and human service system. In "Building Communities From The Inside Out," Kretzman and McKnight lay out a clear, step-by-step process for doing asset assessment to increase individual capacities and to release the power of local associations and organizations. They go on to describe how to capture local institutions for community building, and break that down by parks, schools, libraries, community colleges, hospitals, etc. Finally, the rest of the book focuses on rebuilding a community economy. While you're at it, check out the rest of the publications out of The Center for Urban Affairs and Policy Research, including: Mapping Community Capacity, an earlier version of Building Communities From The Inside Out. Available by writing to: Center for Urban Affairs and Policy Research, Northwestern University, 2040 Sheridan Road, Evanston, IL 60208-4100, Phone: 708-491-8712. Fax: 708-491-9916 $12, p.pd.

8) *Partnerships for Community Development by Sally Habana Hafner and Horace Reed.*

This excellent publication out of the Center for Organizational and Community Development of the University of Massachusetts - Amherst (an organization that followed the Citizen Involvement Training Project, whose publications were also excellent) provides a wonderful overview of partnership behavior and partnerships in general. They distinguish carefully between various types of partnerships, including: networks, coordination and collaboration. Especially helpful in this book are the many exercises for groups to use as they go through the text. It is available from the Center for Organizational and Community Development, 377 Hills South, University of Massachusetts, Amherst, MA 01003, $15.00 plus $2.50 shipping (Bulk discount available).

9) *Organizing for Social Change by Kim Bobo, Jackie Kendall, Steve Max.*

This is a manual for activists in the 1990s and comes from the Midwest Academy, one of the most prestigious organizing training centers in the country. This is focused less on coalition building, and more on direct action, organizing, organizing skills and the steps involved in becoming a good organizer. Well written, clear and an especially helpful manual. Seven Locks Press, P.O. Box 27, Cabin John, MD 20818, $19.95 plus $2 shipping.

10) *Solving Community Problems By Consensus; Facing Racial and Cultural Conflict; and Involving Citizens In Community Decision Making*

These are three excellent manuals all developed by a remarkable man with a remarkable organization - Bill Potapchuk and the Program For Community Problem Solving in Washington, D.C. They have been developing materials and programs to help communities solve problems for many years. These are excellent and usable manuals and in addition to the above titles, there are three volumes of case studies, featuring successful community problem solving, the national directory of problem solving consultants, and a bibliography on building communities. Each of these is attractively designed and well organized with no-nonsense advice and detailed resource lists. For a complete description of materials and prices, contact: The Program For Community Problem Solving, 915 15th Street, NW, 6th Floor, Washington, D.C. 20005, Phone: 202-783-2961.